LegalEats

"What do you do?"   "I'm a lawyer."
                        "The law."
                        "I do law."
                        "I practice law."
                        "I'm an attorney."
                        "Something legal."

LegalEats

A Lawyer's Lite Cookbook

Flavia Joyce Tuzza

Writers Club Press
San Jose New York Lincoln Shanghai

LegalEats
A Lawyer's Lite Cookbook

Writers Club Press
an imprint of iUniverse.com, Inc.

For information address:
iUniverse.com, Inc.
5220 S 16th, Ste. 200
Lincoln, NE 68512
www.iuniverse.com

ISBN: 0-595-14592-2

Printed in the United States of America

DEDICATION

For my parents, John and Josephine Tuzza, with love and gratitude, and for my husband Ira Gleser, the inspiration behind LegalEats.

Epigraph

" For the edible and the readable we give thanks to God, the Author of Life. "

—Mervyn Stockwood

CONTENTS

ACKNOWLEDGEMENTS

LegalEats, A Lawyer's Lite Cookbook has evolved over the years from a simple idea I had about one day writing a fun cookbook targeted to the legal profession to the final product you now see, with the assistance of several people I need to acknowledge and now thank.

First, I want to thank The Cartoon Bank, a Division of *The New Yorker Magazine* for granting me permission to use the cute lawyer cartoons featured in the cookbook. The cartoons are from *The New Yorker Book of Lawyer Cartoons* , a book which continues to make me laugh every time I look at those hilarious cartoons. The hardest part I had in the cartoon selection process was limiting the number of lawyer cartoons I could use due to the budget restraints of this project. The sophisticated brand of humor that *The New Yorker* is famous for was just the thing I was looking for to give *LegalEats* its character and charm.

Next, I want to thank all those non-lawyer creative types whose advice and/or words of encouragement contributed to the making of *LegalEats*, they include my loving husband Ira; Cori, my best pal from childhood, and other talented individuals including freelancers Julie, Melanie, and R.J.

Next, I want to thank Alese who provided technical computer support by entering all the recipes and graphics onto a Zip disk, which was no small task.

Next, there would be no cookbook without all the great-tasting recipes, many of which were adapted from or inspired by the wonderful dishes made over the years by a great lady, namely my mother Josephine Tuzza. She's been cooking light and healthy Mediterranean -style years before it ever became trendy! Thanks Mom for inspiring many of my recipes featured in *LegalEats,* and many thanks for all the life lessons you have taught me and continue to teach me about compassion, courage, caring, giving, loving, faith and strength of character.

Next, I want to acknowledge all those hard working individuals who have devoted their careers to and work within the legal profession. This book's for you! Thank you for your endless contributions and especially to those who help make legal services available to all. I hope by contributing a portion of the profits from the sale of the cookbooks, I can in some small way raise both awareness and funds for various legal services programs while encouraging others to do the same in their own way.

Next, I want to thank all the good folks at iUniverse.com, my publishing partner and cutting-edge, print on demand publisher, for making the publication of *LegalEats* possible.

Finally, very special thanks goes to my husband and resident marketing guru, Ira Gleser for his gift of constant belief, encouragement, technical expertise and time in seeing me through the myriad aspects of this project from start to finish. I also want to thank him for his patience, support and unconditional love that he has shown me as I took time out from the practice of law to complete this project, which he knew was important to me for many reasons. As noted in the cookbook's Dedication page, Ira was the inspiration behind *LegalEats* as well as the one person who has sampled all the recipes and has lived to talk about it!

Lastly, the road to completing this project has taught me some valuable lessons about myself, including the strange notion that there is life after law out there and that the circuitous journey that *LegalEats* has taken me on was well worth it. I encourage all professionals, lawyers and non-lawyers alike, at some point in your careers to take your own "time out" to tap into your creative side, if you have the yearning to do so, just to see where the new road may take you since it just may surprise you.

INTRODUCTION

There are almost one million lawyers in the United States today and they're all hungry! Hence, the need for *LegalEats, A Lawyer's Lite Cookbook*, targeted to members of the legal profession and other lean and mean gourmet types who are looking to lighten up through great tasting recipes and good humor. *LegalEats* is a unique cookbook written by a lawyer for lawyers (and other busy food lovers), whose recipes and tone are on the "light" side. *LegalEats* is the one cookbook that the legal profession can truly call its own. Many of the recipes featured in the cookbook are lighter versions of some old favorites which were given a new twist such as, Legal Lasagna, Counsel's Crab Cakes, Search and Seizure Salad and Libelously Lite Strawberry Cheesecake, just to name a few.

LegalEats makes a perfect and thoughtful gift for all your favorite legal types including but not limited to: lawyers, judges, law clerks, law professors, paralegals, law librarians, law students and legal staff (or anyone else looking to lighten up) since a portion of the author's profits from the sale of the cookbooks will be donated to various legal services programs.

The cookbook's author, Flavia Joyce Tuzza, is a lawyer and gourmet food enthusiast who loves to cook and turn favorite recipes she has collected over the years, into lighter versions without sacrificing great taste. Most of the recipes included are quick, easy and fun to prepare. Flavia believes if it doesn't taste great, why bother? When asked how she knows when she has a great light recipe, Flavia is quick to respond by paraphrasing Justice Potter Stewart's observation on the legal definition of obscenity, "I know it when I see it!" She also believes that contrary to Shakespeare's all too famous line from *Henry VI*, ("let's kill all the lawyers") that we need to give thanks for them and all that they do.

Lastly, whether you spend time in the kitchen, the courtroom, the boardroom, the classroom, the library or the office, remember to keep it light and eat right with *LegalEats* and don't forget to thank a lawyer today! Enjoy!

Opening Statements:
Appetizers, Soups & Salads

"Anyone who tells a lie has not a pure heart, and cannot make a good soup."

—Ludwig van Beethoven

"And should you retain us, Mr. Hodal, you'll find that we're more than just a law firm."

"Laws should be like clothes. They should be made to fit the people they are meant to serve."

—Clarence Darrow

Roman-Style Grilled Cheese Toast

Ingredients:

4   slices, untoasted bread (Italian or French)
     part-skim mozzarella cheese (enough for 4 slices), cut in ½" slices
1   whole egg, beaten (or equivalent egg substitutes)
2   tablespoons water
2-3 tablespoons grated Pecorino cheese
2-3 tablespoons olive oil
     fresh ground black pepper, to taste, optional

- Preheat large non-stick skillet on medium-high heat.
- Cut each slice of bread in half and assemble 4 small bread and cheese sandwiches.
- In a small bowl mix beaten egg, water, grated cheese and pepper, if desired.
- Dip each small cheese sandwich in the egg mixture to coat well like French Toast.
- Add olive oil to hot preheated skillet and lower heat to medium.
- Sauté the small cheese sandwiches in the olive oil a few minutes per side, only until they are golden brown and the cheese begins to melt.
- Drain on paper towels and serve immediately.

Yields: 4 small grilled cheese snacks/appetizers.

Comments: This recipe is a version of a very popular snack commonly found in Rome, Italy. Do not use a lot of olive oil in the skillet or else you will risk deep frying the sandwiches, when they should just be sautéed lightly.

Tomato-Basil Bruschetta

Ingredients:

½ lb. part-skim mozzarella cheese
2-3 plum tomatoes, sliced
1   clove garlic, whole
4   slices crusty bread (Italian or French)
    fresh basil to taste
    salt and fresh ground black pepper, to taste
1-2 tablespoons extra-virgin olive oil

- Toast or grill 4 thick slices of day old crusty bread; rub each slice with the garlic clove.
- Layer on thin slices of mozzarella cheese (at room temperature), tomatoes and top with fresh basil leaves.
- Sprinkle lightly with salt and pepper; then drizzle each serving with olive oil.
- Serve at room temperature.

Yields: 4 tasty appetizers.

Comments: If you like, you can lightly grill the cheese on the toasty bread in the oven before adding the tomatoes, basil and seasonings.

Plaintiff's Pita Chips

Ingredients:

4   whole-wheat pita bread pockets
2   tablespoons extra-virgin olive oil or as needed
    salt, to taste (optional)
    freshly ground black pepper, to taste (optional)
    dash of garlic powder, to taste (optional)

- Preheat oven to 300 degrees.
- Slice pita pockets in half, then quarters, then eighths and peel each piece apart.
- Lightly brush both sides of pita pieces with olive oil and sprinkle each piece with salt, pepper and garlic powder, to taste, if desired.
- Arrange pita pieces into a single layer on a cookie sheet and bake until golden brown and crisp for about 7 to 10 minutes. Transfer to paper towels to cool.

Yields: About 4 servings.

Comments: These pita chips burn very easily so do not bake them at high temperatures. Use them as an appetizer or snack to serve with salsa or a favorite spread such as Hummus, or serve them in salads as a topping in place of croutons or bread.

Habeas Hummus (a/k/a Chick-Pea Spread)

Ingredients:

4   cups (about 2½ cans) garbanzos or chick-peas, drained
$1/3$ cup water
$1/3$ cup extra-virgin olive oil
      juice of 2 lemons
3   cloves garlic
$1^1/2$ teaspoons salt
2   teaspoons ground cumin
      freshly ground black pepper, to taste

- Combine chick-peas, water, olive oil and lemon juice in a food processor or blender.
- Process until smooth.
- Add garlic, salt, cumin and black pepper to taste.
- Process to blend ingredients.
- Remove to a covered container and refrigerate until ready to serve.

Yields: About 1 quart.

Comments: This Middle-Eastern dish is a good companion to homemade pita chips for an appetizer or a snack. Note that this spread can be made ahead in large batches and refrigerated until ready to use.

Crostini With Pesto and Feta

Ingredients:

1   loaf Italian or French Bread
1   bunch fresh bail, or to taste
1   teaspoon minced garlic
¼   cup olive oil
1   tablespoon grated imported Parmesan cheese
1   tablespoon pine nuts (optional)
½   pound low-fat feta cheese
     freshly ground black pepper, to taste

- Preheat oven to 350 degrees.
- Section bread in 1/4 inch slices.
- Combine all the other ingredients, except the feta cheese, in a processor and blend for 30 seconds.
- Spread the mixture over the bread slices. Top each piece with a slice of feta cheese. Bake for 7 to 10 minutes.

Yields: 6 servings.

Comments: You can serve these crispy edibles as an appetizer or as part of a dinner buffet.

"I don't know if I want a lawyer to tell me what I cannot do. I hire him to tell me how to do what I want to do."

—J. P. Morgan

Quick and Hearty Minestrone Soup

Ingredients:

5-6 cups vegetable or chicken broth, low sodium and non-fat
1   yellow onion, chopped
1   clove garlic, minced
4   celery stalks, chopped coarsely
¼   cup parsley, chopped
¼   teaspoon dried oregano
2   tomatoes, chopped coarsely
1   cup cooked small macaroni
1   can (1 pound 4 ounces) chick-peas or garbanzos, drained
     freshly ground black pepper, to taste
     grated imported Parmesan cheese, to garnish (optional)

- Into a container of either a blender or food processor, put ½ cup broth, onion, garlic, celery, parsley, herbs and seasonings.
- Cover, blend or process for about 10 seconds.
- Pour into a saucepan.
- Add remaining broth. Simmer, covered for about 20 minutes.
- Into a container of processor put tomatoes. Cover and process only until tomatoes are coarsely chopped.
- Add to soup mixture.
- Add macaroni and chick-peas. Heat well.
- Add any additional seasonings to taste.
- Serve hot, sprinkled with grated Parmesan cheese, if desired.

Yields: Approximately 6 servings.

Comments: This is the fastest way to prepare this traditional favorite in a most non-traditional way. Add a salad or sandwich on the side to make a complete meal with this hearty dish or serve alone with some good crusty bread on the side. Freeze any leftovers for future use.

Beneficiary's Broccoli Soup

Ingredients:

1   large head of broccoli or 2 smaller heads
2-3   cloves garlic, minced
2-3   tablespoons extra-virgin olive oil
4   cups chicken broth (low-sodium and non-fat)
¼   cup uncooked rice
      freshly ground black pepper, to taste
      grated imported Parmesan cheese, to garnish (optional)

- Heat olive oil in a large saucepan and sauté garlic for about a minute.
- Break apart broccoli by separating flowerets and stalks. Remove tough skin off stalks with sharp knife and chop stalks into ½ -inch cubes.
- Add cubed stalks to sautéed garlic and stir in ¼ cup uncooked rice and stir well. *To Blanche Broccoli Flowerets*: In a saucepan, boil several cups of water and add broccoli flowerets and boil for only 3 minutes until bright green in color. Drain flowerets into a colander and rinse under cold water to stop the cooking process. Set aside flowerets.
- Add 4 cups chicken broth to broccoli-rice-garlic mixture and heat well and bring to a boil. Cover and heat for another 15-20 minutes until rice is cooked.
- Remove cover and spoon out mixture into a food processor or blender and puree a little at a time. Return all the pureed soup back to soup pan and heat thoroughly.

- Add freshly ground black pepper, to taste. Add back into the soup, the broccoli flowerets and serve hot. Sprinkle each serving with grated Parmesan, if desired.

Comments: This makes a great light first course to any meal, and can be made ahead and re-heated. As with most soups, you can also freeze any leftovers.

Easy Egg Drop Noodle Soup

Ingredients:

1	green onion, chopped
½	cup parsley, chopped
1	clove garlic, minced
2	tablespoons olive oil
1	egg, well beaten
1	quart chicken broth (low sodium and non-fat)
2	tablespoons soy sauce
8	ounces wide noodles, cooked al dente or slightly undercooked and drained
	freshly ground black pepper and salt, to taste (optional)
	grated imported Parmesan cheese, to garnish (optional)

- In a deep pot or saucepan, heat olive oil and sauté onions and garlic for a few minutes, stirring occasionally. Beat egg in a small bowl and set aside.
- Add 1 quart chicken broth to pot with onion and garlic. Stir and heat thoroughly until chicken broth comes to a full boil.
- Gradually stir in egg mixture until strings form, then add soy sauce and bring back to a full boil.
- Add parsley, salt, black pepper and cooked noodles and bring back to full boil long enough to heat soup and noodles thoroughly.
- Serve hot and sprinkle each serving with grated Parmesan, if desired.

Yields: Approximately 6 servings.

Comments: This soup can be made ahead in larger batches over the week-end, then just re-heat when you are ready to use. For those who prefer a more traditional egg drop soup, just omit the noodles. However, this soup made with the noodles can be turned into a complete meal by just adding a salad on the side.

Squash Subpoena Soup
(a/k/a Butternut Squash Soup)

Ingredients:

1	tablespoon olive oil
1	onion, diced
3	carrots, diced
3	celery stalks, diced
1	large clove garlic, minced
¼-½	teaspoon ground ginger
7-8	cups chicken broth (low sodium and non-fat)
4	cups 1-inch cubes butternut squash
3	medium potatoes, peeled and sliced
½	teaspoon salt, or to taste
½	teaspoon freshly ground black pepper, or to taste
1	carrot, finely grated in food processor, set aside for garnish
	dash of garlic powder, to taste (optional)
¼-½	cup finely chopped green onions or chives, for garnish

- Heat the olive oil in a large soup pot over medium heat. Add the diced onion, carrots, celery and garlic; sauté, stirring frequently, until the onion is tender and translucent, about 5 minutes.
- Add the ginger and sauté for another minute. Add the broth, squash cubes and potatoes. Bring the soup to a full boil over medium heat, then reduce the heat to low and simmer until the squash is tender, for about 20 minutes.
- Remove the soup from the heat and allow it to cool, 15 to 20 minutes.

- Puree the soup in several small batches in a food processor or blender.
- Return the soup to the pot and add grated carrot. Bring soup back up to a boil. Adjust seasoning to taste.
- Garnish soup with chives or green onions.

Yields: Approximately 10 servings.

Comments: This is a good soup for the fall or winter months. Try it as a first course to a traditional Thanksgiving dinner or serve it during the week with a salad on the side for a quick meatless main dish. Make it in large batches and after cooling, store in covered containers in the refrigerator or freezer and pull out during the week when you are ready to use it.

Litigator's Lentil Soup

Ingredients:

2   tablespoons olive oil
1   onion, chopped
1   celery stalk, chopped
1   carrot, chopped
1   clove garlic, minced
2   large tomatoes, chopped
1$^1/_4$ cups ($^1/_2$ pound) lentils, rinsed
6   cups chicken broth (low sodium and non-fat)
1   large head escarole (1 pound), cleaned and chopped
     grated imported Parmesan cheese, to taste for garnish (optional)
     dash of salt, to taste (optional)
     freshly ground black pepper, to taste

* In a large soup or stockpot, heat oil over medium heat. Add onion, celery and carrot. Cook, stirring frequently until the vegetables are soft and tender, 8 to 10 minutes.
* Stir in garlic and escarole and cook covered for another few minutes until escarole is wilted.
* Add tomatoes, reduce the heat to low and cook, stirring often, for 5 minutes longer.
* Add lentils and 6 cups of broth to the pot. Bring to a simmer and cook, partially covered, until the lentils are tender, about 45 minutes.
* Season lightly with salt and pepper, to taste, if desired.

• Serve hot in individual bowls and sprinkle each serving bowl lightly with some grated Parmesan cheese, if desired.

Yields: 4-6 servings.

Comments: Like many soup recipes, this soup actually tastes better the next day, so it can be made ahead and stored covered in the refrigerator until ready to serve.

Spinach Soup Supreme

Ingredients:

¾   pound fresh spinach, washed and trimmed or 10 ounce package
       frozen spinach, prepared according to package instructions
5-6   cups or 3 cans (14$\frac{1}{2}$ ounces each) chicken broth
       (low sodium, fat-free)
2   medium onions, chopped
3   stalks celery, chopped
1   large clove garlic, minced
2   tablespoons olive oil
3   large potatoes, peeled and chopped
½   teaspoon salt or to taste
½   teaspoon freshly ground black pepper or to taste
¼   cup chopped green onions, for garnish (optional)
       garlic powder, to taste (optional)

- In a large saucepan or stockpot, heat the olive oil. Over medium heat, sauté the onions for a few minutes. Add the celery and garlic and continue to sauté for 2 to 3 minutes longer, stirring occasionally.
- Add the potatoes and sauté for 2 to 3 minutes longer.
- Pour in the chicken broth, lower the heat and simmer until the potatoes are tender, about 20-25 minutes.
- Blanche fresh spinach or prepare frozen spinach according to package directions. Drain and squeeze out liquid. Chop spinach coarsely.
- Add ½ the amount of spinach to soup.

- Allow soup to cool down to room temperature. Puree the soup in small portions in a blender or food processor. Return the soup to the pot and re-heat soup.
- Break up the remaining ½ of spinach and stir into the soup.
- Season with salt, pepper and garlic powder, if desired, to taste.
- Heat over a low flame until soup is hot.
- Ladle soup into bowls and garnish with green onions, if desired.

Yields: 6-8 servings.

Comments: Like most homemade soups, this recipe can be made ahead and stored in a covered container in the refrigerator or freezer. Just re-heat when ready to serve.

Common-Law Corn Chowder

Ingredients:

1	tablespoon olive oil
2	medium yellow onions, chopped (about 2 cups)
1	tablespoon garlic puree or about 6 cloves, chopped
2	large potatoes, peeled and chopped
½	teaspoon salt or to taste
	freshly ground black pepper, to taste
½	teaspoon ground cumin
½	teaspoon dried thyme leaves
3	cans (14½ ounces each) fat-free low-sodium chicken broth
1½	cups skim milk
2	cups water
1	(16-ounce) bag frozen whole-kernel corn

- In a large pot, heat the oil over medium heat. Add the onions and garlic and cook slowly, about 3-5 minutes.
- Add the chopped potatoes along with the salt, pepper, cumin and thyme. Combine ingredients evenly with the onions and garlic and cook, stirring well for about 1 minute.
- Stir in the chicken broth, water and skim milk and bring to a boil. Add corn and reduce heat to simmer. Cover pot and continue to simmer for an additional 20 minutes, until potatoes and corn are tender; stir occasionally to prevent sticking.
- Uncover pot and allow chowder to cool down about 10 minutes before you puree the vegetables in a blender or food processor, just for a few

seconds. [The chowder should be of a thick, slightly lumpy consistency.] If too thick, thin with water and adjust seasonings.

- Re-heat in pot or in the microwave and serve hot.

Yields: Approximately 6 servings.

Wild Witness Rice Soup

Ingredients:

1   tablespoon olive oil
2   yellow onions, chopped
3   carrots, chopped
6   cloves garlic, chopped (or 1 tablespoon garlic puree)
1   cup uncooked wild rice and 3 cups water
2   cans (14½ ounces each) or about 5-6 cups chicken broth (fat-free, low sodium type)
1   cup water
3   potatoes, peeled and chopped
     parsley or chives, minced for garnish
     salt and freshly ground black pepper, to taste
     favorite fresh herbs for soup (such as thyme or ½ teaspoon dried thyme leaves)

To Make Wild Rice:

Wash uncooked wild rice thoroughly. Combine 1 cup rice and 3 cups water and ½ teaspoon salt (optional) in a heavy saucepan. Bring to boil. Reduce heat to low boil, cover loosely and cook for approximately 45 minutes until most of liquid is absorbed. Set aside.

• Heat olive oil in large saucepan or soup pan and sauté onions until tender. Add garlic and chopped carrots and sauté another few minutes. Add potatoes and thyme, cook another few minutes.

- Add chicken broth, bring to a boil and simmer, covered on low heat about 20 minutes until potatoes are very tender.
- Uncover soup and allow to cool about 10-15 minutes before you puree soup in small batches in a food processor or blender.
- Return pureed soup to pot and re-heat to bring back to a boil. Add cooked rice and seasonings, to taste.
- Garnish with fresh minced parsley or chives.

Yields: 8-10 servings.

Trustee's Tomato Soup

Ingredients:

6   cups sliced potatoes (5-6 medium potatoes)
1   tablespoon olive oil
2   cups chopped yellow onions
5   large garlic cloves, minced
1   cup diced celery
1   cup diced carrots
½   teaspoon dried thyme
1   teaspoon dried basil
1   cup skim milk
1   teaspoon salt
1   (28-ounce) can peeled and crushed tomatoes with their juice
     homemade croutons, for garnish (optional)

- Bring 2 cups water to a boil in a saucepan and cook the potatoes until tender, about 15-20 minutes.
- Heat the oil in a large skillet over medium heat. Sauté the onions, garlic, celery, carrot, thyme and basil until vegetables are tender, about 7-10 minutes.
- Remove the pot from the heat. Working in small batches, puree the potatoes, their cooking water and the skim milk in a blender or food processor.
- Stir the puree into a soup pot, along with the salt, tomatoes and their juices, sautéed vegetables and 3 more cups of water. Bring the soup to a

simmer and cook 15 minutes, stirring occasionally. Ladle into individual soup bowls and top with homemade croutons, if desired. Serve hot.

Yields: Approximately 8-10 servings.

Comments: Homemade croutons can be easily made with any of your favorite (untoasted) day old French or Italian bread. Cut bread into a few slices and then into ½-inch cubes. Mix cubed bread with a tablespoon or two of extra-virgin olive oil, freshly ground black pepper and dash of garlic powder in a bowl until all ingredients are well combined. Spread into a single layer onto an ungreased baking sheet and bake in 250-300 degree oven for about 8-10 minutes each side. Watch for burning. Remove croutons from oven and allow to cool completely before using in salads or soups.

Timely Tuscan Soup

Ingredients:

2-4   tablespoons olive oil
1   cup chopped carrots
1   cup chopped onions
1   cup chopped celery
2   garlic cloves, minced
1   (19-ounce) can Cannellini beans, drained, rinsed
1   (15-ounce) can black beans, drained, rinsed
2   (14.5-ounce) cans low-sodium, non-fat chicken broth
½   teaspoon dried thyme leaves
      small bunch fresh oregano, basil or cilantro, chopped
6   fresh plum tomatoes, chopped
      salt and fresh ground black pepper, to taste
      2 cups cold water
      grated Pecorino or Parmesan cheese for garnish, optional
      homemade croutons for garnish, optional

- In a large soup pot, heat oil over medium-high heat.
- Add carrots, onions, celery and garlic; cook 5-7 minutes until onions are tender, stir occasionally.
- Add chicken broth and water; heat for a few minutes.
- Stir in thyme leaves and add your favorite fresh herbs and tomatoes.
- Stir in beans, cover and simmer soup on low heat for about 20-30 minutes; season to taste.
- Garnish with homemade croutons and freshly grated cheese, if desired.

Yields: 6-8 servings.

Comments: This is a very quick homemade soup to prepare when using the canned beans.

"The sound of tireless voices is the price we pay for the right to hear the music of our own opinions."

—Adlai Stevenson

Tuscan Tomato Bread Salad

Ingredients:

4   cups large fresh plum/roma tomatoes, diced
1   large red onion, slivered (optional)
½   cup water
¹/₃ cup extra virgin olive oil
¼   cup balsamic vinegar
    dash of ground black pepper and garlic powder, to taste
    dash of salt and crumbled feta cheese, to taste
½   cup minced fresh basil or oregano
6   cups crusty bread, cut into 1-inch cubes

- Combine the tomatoes, onion, water, olive oil, vinegar, pepper, salt, garlic powder and basil, and let stand for 10 minutes.
- Add bread and crumbled cheese, and toss well to coat just prior to serving.
- Do not refrigerate.

Yields: Approximately 4 servings.

Comments: This makes a great summer salad/appetizer in place of the traditional green salad.

Veggie Potato Salad

Ingredients:

2½ pounds red skin potatoes
¼ cup balsamic vinegar
1 tablespoon Dijon mustard
1 clove garlic, minced
¾ cup chopped red or green onion
1/3 cup fresh parsley or cilantro, minced
1 package frozen corn or mixed veggies
¼ cup extra virgin olive oil
    salt, freshly ground pepper and
    crumbled feta cheese, to taste

- Put potatoes in large pot and add cold water to just cover.
- Bring to a simmer over medium heat and cook until tender (about 20 minutes).
- Prepare frozen corn or mixed veggies according to microwave directions, run under cold water, drain and set aside.
- Drain potatoes and run under cold water until they are cool enough to handle.
- Cut into large diced chunks and sprinkle with 2 tablespoons of the vinegar.
- In a bowl whisk olive oil, remaining vinegar, mustard, salt and pepper.
- Add dressing to the potatoes and toss well.
- Add onions and parsley or cilantro and toss again.

- Heat 2 tablespoons of olive oil in large skillet and add cooked well-drained corn or mixed veggies and roast in skillet with garlic for a few minutes on medium heat until lightly browned.
- Add roasted corn or mixed veggies to potato mixture and toss again, and sprinkle with any additional salt, pepper and feta cheese, to taste.

Yields: Approximately 6 servings.

Comments: This dish can be made several hours ahead before serving and allowed to sit at room temperature. It also makes a great potato salad without the roasted veggies.

Green Beans and Feta Salad

Ingredients:

1½ pounds fresh green beans, trimmed and halved
¾ cup extra-virgin olive oil
½ cup fresh basil, finely chopped
½ cup balsamic vinegar
2 cloves garlic, minced
1 medium red onion, chopped
1 cup low-fat feta cheese
   dash of salt, to taste (optional)
   freshly ground black pepper, to taste

- Boil beans in a saucepan of lightly salted water until crispy and tender, for about 5 minutes. Drain, then rinse with cold water. Drain again, pat dry and set aside.
- Combine oil, basil, vinegar, salt, if desired, garlic and black pepper for dressing.
- In a separate bowl, combine beans, red onion and cheese. Add dressing and toss together thoroughly before serving.

Yields: About 6 servings.

Comments: This makes a great side dish to any grilled seafood or chicken entree. It also can be made ahead, refrigerated and taken to cookouts or picnics since it also travels well.

Ruling Rice and Bean Salad

Ingredients:

1	tablespoon lime juice
2	tablespoons (extra virgin) olive oil
¾	teaspoon chili powder
¾	teaspoon garlic powder
½	cup brown rice
1	15-ounce can black beans, rinsed and drained
¼	cup minced green onion
½	cup chopped green bell pepper
½	cup chopped red bell pepper
½	cup chopped yellow bell pepper
¼	cup chopped fresh cilantro
¼	cup low-fat cheddar cheese or Monterey jack (optional)

- In a small bowl, mix lime juice, oil, chili powder and garlic powder; set dressing aside.
- In a medium saucepan, cook rice according to package directions. Stir in saucepan with cooked rice, black beans, onion, peppers and cilantro.
- Pour dressing over salad.
- Serve warm and sprinkled with cheese, if desired.

Yields: 4 servings.

Comments: Try serving this tasty Southwestern dish with warmed whole wheat tortillas on the side as a main dish salad.

Search & Seizure Salad Dressing

Ingredients:

     juice of 1 fresh lemon
$1/3$ cup extra virgin olive oil
3   tablespoons Dijon mustard
1   tablespoon balsamic vinegar
3   tablespoons, grated imported Parmesan or
     Romano cheese (or to taste)
½   teaspoon freshly grated black pepper (or to taste)
     dash of garlic powder, to taste
     dash of salt, to taste (optional)

- In a small bowl, add lemon juice and whisk in the mustard, vinegar, garlic powder and black pepper until thoroughly combined. Slowly whisk in the olive oil.
- Lastly, add the grated cheese. Taste and adjust seasonings, if necessary.
- Toss over a head of romaine lettuce and serve immediately.

Yields: Dressing for 1 head of lettuce.

Comments: For a variation, add chopped or sliced leftover grilled chicken to the Romaine lettuce for a quick warm weather chicken Caesar-type salad entrée.

"The meek shall inherit the earth, but not the mineral rights."
—J. Paul Getty

MAIN ARGUMENTS:
ENTREES & CASSEROLES

"The one great principle of the English law is to make business for itself."

—Charles Dickens

"Never serve oysters in a month that has no paycheck in it."
—P. J. O'Rourke

Counsel's Crab Cakes

Ingredients:

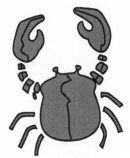

6   ounces crab meat, special lump white meat
1   egg or egg substitutes
2   tablespoons non-fat or light mayonnaise
1   tablespoon Dijon mustard
1   teaspoon fresh lemon juice
2   tablespoons green onions, chopped
3-4 tablespoons fresh cilantro, chopped
2   tablespoons grated imported Parmesan or Romano cheese
    freshly ground black pepper, to taste
    dash of garlic powder, to taste (optional)
¼   cup seasoned Italian breadcrumbs
3-4 tablespoons olive oil

- In a large mixing bowl, add crabmeat and remaining ingredients, except the oil, and mix well.
- Form the mixture into 4 large or 6 small crab cakes.
- In a large non-stick skillet, heat the olive oil. Sauté the crab cakes for a few minutes on each side until golden brown. Drain on paper towels.

Yields: 2-4 servings.

Comments: Garnish crab cakes with lemon or lime wedges and serve with or over a large green salad for a great warm weather dinner or serve with a small green salad on the side, with a baked potato.

Practitioner's Paella

Ingredients:

1   package (10 oz.) yellow rice mix
½   pound jumbo shrimp, peeled and rinsed
¾   pound red snapper or amberjack fillet (or any firm fish fillet)
1   pound white meat chicken fillets, cut into bite size chunks
1½ pounds mussels in shell
1   stalk green onion, chopped
½   cup fresh cilantro, chopped
1   medium yellow onion, chopped
1   clove garlic, minced
1½ cups white wine (not cooking wine)
3-4 plum tomatoes, diced
3-4 tablespoons extra virgin olive oil
½   cup non-fat, low sodium chicken broth
      freshly ground black pepper and salt, to taste

- Prepare rice according to directions on package and set aside.
- In large non-stick frying pan, sauté green onions, garlic, and yellow onion until soft in approximately 2-3 tablespoons heated olive oil; remove from pan and add chicken and cook until well browned on each side.
- Remove chicken from pan and set aside.
- Return sautéed onions and garlic to pan and add fish fillet. Sauté on medium heat, turning occasionally, and add ½ cup white wine and cover. Cook for approximately 5 minutes until tender. Do not overcook.

- Add cooked rice mixture and all other cooked ingredients plus chicken broth, and stir thoroughly. Reduce heat to low.
- Add chopped cilantro and stir. Add additional 1 cup white wine and mussels, cover, and cook on low to medium heat for 10 minutes until mussels have opened and mixture is thoroughly heated.
- Add chopped tomatoes and heat another 2-3 minutes; stir thoroughly.
- Lastly, add shrimp to mixture, mix well so shrimp are on the bottom of the pan. Cook covered, for another 3-4 minutes until shrimp are pink and just cooked.
- Add salt and pepper to taste and serve immediately.

Yields: Approximately 4 servings.

Comments: For those who enjoy a more traditional paella taste, add chopped, cooked chorizo sausage at the end and mix in with other ingredients. Many thanks to my husband, Ira who prepares this dish for us.

Fiduciary's Fish Fillets

Ingredients:

4   firm, fresh fish fillets (such as flounder, sole, grouper,
     red snapper or sea bass), approximately 6 ounces each
¾   cup seasoned Italian breadcrumbs
1   egg, beaten or egg white or egg substitute, plus 2 tablespoons water
2   tablespoons olive oil
     nonstick cooking spray
     lemon wedges, to garnish

- Preheat oven to 375 degrees.
- Beat egg and water in a large bowl.
- Dip cleaned and dry fish fillets, one at a time, in egg mixture, then dip each fish fillet in seasoned breadcrumbs.
- Line a baking dish with aluminum foil and coat with nonstick cooking spray.
- Place each breaded fillet in a single layer in baking dish. Drizzle fillets lightly with a little olive oil over each top.
- Bake approximately 15-20 minutes, depending on thickness of fish, until golden brown.
- Remove from baking dish to serving plates and garnish with lemon wedges.

Yields: 4 servings.

Comments: Serve with a green salad on the side, along with some fresh stir-fry veggies or steamed vegetables such as broccoli or green beans.

Shrimp Over Penne Pesto

Ingredients:

¼	pound uncooked penne pasta
2	tablespoons dry white wine
1	green onion, chopped
8-10	large shrimp, peeled, deveined and halved lengthwise
1	tablespoon water
1	tablespoon balsamic vinegar
½	teaspoon salt (optional)
1	recipe Lite Pesto Sauce *(see recipe)*

- Cook the pasta according to package directions.
- While the pasta is cooking, place white wine in a large non-stick skillet and bring to a boil.
- Add the shrimp, water, balsamic vinegar, salt and cook just until shrimp have turned pink. Do not overcook shrimp.
- Remove from heat. Drain the pasta and place in a large bowl.
- Add the Lite Pesto Sauce, to the shrimp and toss to coat evenly.
- Serve immediately.

Yields: 2 servings.

Comments: Serve with a small green salad on the side along with some Low-Fat Garlic Bread *(see recipe)*.

Lawyer's Linguine With Tomatoes and Shrimp

Ingredients:

½ pound large shrimp (cleaned, peeled, deveined and cut in half lengthwise)

2 tablespoons extra-virgin olive oil

4 tablespoons fresh basil, minced

4 plum tomatoes, diced

1/3 cup green onion, chopped

1 large clove garlic, minced

3 tablespoons dry white wine
dash of salt (optional)
freshly ground black pepper, to taste
grated imported Parmesan cheese (optional)

- Cook linguine according to package directions.
- While linguine is cooking, heat olive oil in a large non-stick skillet and sauté onion and garlic for a few minutes.
- Add tomatoes, basil, white wine, salt, if desired, and black pepper and cook for about 3 to 4 minutes.
- Add shrimp and cook for about 2-3 minutes just until shrimp begin to turn pink. Do not overcook shrimp.
- Drain cooked linguine and pour into a platter. Top with shrimp and tomato mixture and toss lightly. Sprinkle with grated Parmesan, if desired.

Yields: 2 servings.

Comments: Serve with a small green salad on the side and some Low-Fat Garlic Bread *(see recipe)*, if desired.

"Nothing conduces to brevity like a caving in of the knees."
—Oliver Wendell Holmes, Jr.

Slanderous Shrimp Fra Diavolo with Penne Pasta

Ingredients:

15   ounces of penne pasta
1   tablespoon extra virgin olive oil
1   small yellow onion, minced
¼   teaspoon salt
¼   teaspoon crushed red pepper or freshly ground black pepper (more or less to taste)
1   28-ounce can diced plum tomatoes in puree
1   lb. cleaned, medium or large shrimp
2   cloves minced garlic
1   bunch of fresh chopped basil, (optional)

- Cook pasta according to package directions.
- Meanwhile: In a large nonstick skillet heat the olive oil, and cook minced onion for about 3 minutes. Add garlic, salt, crushed red pepper or black pepper and cook for another minute.
- Add diced plum tomatoes in puree and heat to boiling. Cook for 5 minutes longer.
- Stir in shrimp and basil, if desired, cook 3-4 minutes or until shrimp turn opaque.

Yields: Approximately 4 servings.

Comments: Serve with a green salad and crusty bread on the side. Instead of the penne pasta, substitute with your favorite pasta.

Pan-Seared Salmon with Tomatoes

Ingredients:

4   firm-fleshed fish fillets (approximately 6 ounces each) such as salmon, grouper or sea bass
6-8 plum tomatoes, diced
    salt and ground pepper, to taste
¼   cup fresh basil, chopped
2   cloves garlic, minced
½   cup dry white wine
2-3 tablespoons olive oil, extra virgin

- Rinse fish fillets and pat dry.
- Heat heavy stick-resistant skillet over high heat until very hot.
- Add oil, heat briefly.
- Add fish & cook turning several times, approximately 5 minutes.
- Add tomatoes, then garlic and cook for about 2-3 minutes longer.
- Add the wine, basil, salt and pepper to taste. Simmer, covered for another 3-4 minutes.
- Serve hot over pasta or serve along with some crusty bread.

Yields: 4 servings.

Mediator's Mussells & Linguine

Ingredients:

1   pound fresh mussells (cleaned and debearded)
16   ounces uncooked linguine
1   large onion, chopped
4-6 plum tomatoes, quartered
½   cup fresh basil, chopped
2   cloves garlic, minced
1   cup dry white wine
3-4 tablespoons olive oil, divided
     freshly grated Parmesan cheese (optional topping)

- Clean and rinse mussels, set aside.
- Sauté onions in 2 tablespoons olive oil in a large non-stick skillet; add garlic and continue cooking until onions wilted.
- Add tomatoes and basil and continue cooking a few minutes longer until tomatoes soften.
- Add white wine to skillet and cook entire mixture until it begins to boil. Add mussels to skillet, cover and steam for approximately 7 minutes, until all mussels have opened.
- Cook linguine according to its package instructions while the mussels are steaming.
- Discard any unopened mussels after the steaming time is over. Drain pasta, sprinkle with remaining olive oil and toss lightly to prevent sticking.
- Top pasta with mussels and its "sauce" from skillet; toss all lightly and sprinkle with grated cheese, if desired.

Yields: Approximately 4 servings.

Grilled Salmon with Dill

Ingredients:

¾-1 lb. thick salmon fillets or salmon steaks
    juice of 1 lime
2-3 tablespoons extra virgin olive oil
1   tablespoon Dijon mustard
    garlic powder, salt and freshly ground pepper, to taste
    small bunch freshly chopped dill or cilantro
    lime wedges for garnish, optional

For Marinade:
- Whisk together lime juice, olive oil and Dijon mustard. Add remaining seasonings and fresh dill (or cilantro). Stir well.
- Pour marinade over salmon in a covered dish and set aside at room temperature for no longer than 15 minutes.

To Grill:
- Preheat outdoor grill on medium-high heat.
- Grill approximately 4 minutes per side on medium heat.
- Serve immediately.
- Garnish with lime wedges, if desired.

Yields: 2 servings.

"As one gets older, litigation replaces sex."

—Gore Vidal

Magistrate's Mushroom Chili

Ingredients:

2   tablespoons olive oil

2   lbs. assorted mushrooms (crimini, portabello and white mushrooms) rinsed, patted dry and chopped

1   large onion, chopped

2   garlic cloves, minced

1   green bell pepper, cored, seeded and chopped

2   tablespoons chopped jalapeño chili peppers

2   tablespoons dried oregano

1   tablespoon paprika

1   tablespoon cumin

1   teaspoon cayenne pepper

    hot sauce, to taste (optional)

1   (28 ounce) can crushed tomatoes

3   (1 lb.) cans red kidney beans, rinsed & drained

    salt and fresh ground black pepper, to taste

- In a large skillet, heat oil over medium heat. Add mushrooms, onion, garlic and peppers; cook stirring until most of liquid is absorbed, 8 to 10 minutes.
- Add oregano, paprika, cumin, cayenne, hot sauce if desired, salt and pepper. Stir until vegetables are soft, about 6-7 minutes. Stir in tomatoes and beans.
- Bring to just a boil. Reduce heat and cook, partially covered for 15 minutes.

Yields: 9 cups (which can be frozen until ready to use).

Comments: Suggested toppings include salsa, chopped tomatoes, shredded low-fat cheese or chopped scallions.

Ruling Ribollita (Tuscan Bean & Vegetable Stew)

Ingredients:

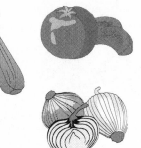

1   pound uncooked white beans
2/3   cup onions, diced
2/3   cup carrots, diced
2/3   cup celery, diced
2   cloves garlic, minced
4-5   plum tomatoes, diced
4-5   cans of non-fat low sodium chicken or vegetable stock
        assorted bunch of fresh herbs (such as parsley, basil & oregano)
3   tablespoons olive oil
        fresh parmigiano cheese, grated (to taste)
        several slices of crusty bread, cubed
        salt and freshly ground pepper (to taste)

- Wash white beans well by rinsing several times in cold water or soak beans overnight.
- Add washed beans to large stock pot, cover with water and bring to a boil. Remove pot from heat and allow beans to sit in water several hours to soften.
- Add more water to cover and simmer until beans are tender but not mushy.
- Sauté onions, carrots, celery and garlic in olive oil for about 10-12 minutes.
- Add tomatoes and cooked beans; pour in the stock and simmer for approximately 1 hour.

- Add bread cubes, fresh minced herbs and seasoning to taste and let stand for another hour before reheating, and serving with grated cheese on top.

Yields: Lots of Stew! (several quarts)

Comments: This dish also tastes great with many types of leftovers added to it such as, cooked pasta, rice, potatoes, and countless green vegetables, giving this dish a stew-like consistency. This recipe yields many portions, which can vary depending on the amount of bread, stock and leftovers added to it.

Background of Recipe: My version of this classic Tuscan dish was inspired by a trip to Italy, where one can find many variations of this traditional thick veggie, bean and bread soup in the Tuscany region. In Italy, Ribollita is often served as a "primi piatti" (first course) but since it is so hearty, I found you can enjoy it as a great meat-less main dish for dinner, served with a green salad on the side. It also makes a great fall and winter hearty lunch. Since Tuscan cooks are known for their creative use of leftovers, no two versions of Ribollita tastes exactly the same, which is part of the fun of this wonderful dish!

"Laws and institutions are constantly tending to gravitate. Like clocks, they must be occasionally cleansed, and wound up, and set to true time."

—Henry Ward Beecher

Solicitor's Lite Spinach Quiche

Ingredients:

2   whole eggs, plus egg substitutes equal
     to 2 whole eggs
8   ounces lite Swiss cheese, shredded
4   tablespoons light or non-fat mayonnaise
1   package (10 ounces) frozen spinach
1   tablespoon olive oil
4   tablespoons grated imported cheese
     (Parmesan or Romano)
     freshly ground black pepper and salt, to taste
1   cup skim milk
1   frozen 9-inch deep dish pie shell
     Dash of garlic powder, to taste

- Preheat oven to 350 degrees.
- Prepare frozen spinach according to microwave directions on package, rinse spinach under cold water to cool, and drain well with paper towels.
- Season spinach with olive oil, and dash of garlic powder, salt and pepper, and set aside.
- Beat eggs slightly and mix in remaining ingredients, adding seasoned spinach last.
- Pour egg mixture into pie shell.
- Sprinkle grated cheese on top and bake for 15 minutes at 350 degrees.
- Reduce heat to 300 degrees and bake for 30-35 additional minutes.

- Remove from oven and let stand 10-15 minutes at room temperature.
- Slice and serve in pie wedges.

Yields: Approximately 6 servings.

Comments: You will find that this dish also tastes great left over the next day. To re-heat, microwave each serving approximately one minute on high power.

Shitake Mushroom and Basil Frittata

Ingredients:

6   eggs (or equivalent egg substitutes)

½   cup finely chopped green onions

²/3   cup thinly sliced Shitake mushrooms

¹/3   cup minced fresh basil (or cilantro)

½   cup imported grated Parmesan cheese divided (¼ cup for mixture and ¼ cup for topping)

2   tablespoons extra virgin olive oil

1   teaspoon freshly ground black pepper, or to taste

- Whisk together eggs, ¼ cup grated Parmesan cheese and black pepper. Set aside.
- Heat oil in a 10-inch ovenproof skillet over medium heat. Add green onions and cook, stirring until onions soften, about 2 minutes. Add mushrooms and basil and continue cooking 2-3 minutes longer.
- Add egg mixture; cook until eggs begin to set at edges. Using a spatula, lift cooked eggs and tilt pan so uncooked eggs flow from center to edges. Continue to cook until eggs are just softly set in center, about 3-4 minutes.
- Sprinkle remaining ¼ cup grated Parmesan cheese over top and transfer to a heated broiler. Broil just until eggs are set, no longer than 2 minutes. Do not overcook. Remove from oven.
- Turn over into a serving plate and slice into wedges. Serve immediately.

Yields: 4 servings.

Lean and Mean Meatballs

Ingredients:

12   ounces extra-lean ground beef or ground turkey
¼   cup Italian seasoned dried breadcrumbs
1   egg white (or egg substitute equal to 1 whole egg)
2   tablespoons chopped fresh oregano or ½ teaspoon dried oregano
3   cups low-fat tomato sauce
3   tablespoons Parmesan cheese, grated
      dash of garlic powder
2   tablespoons chopped fresh parsley or basil
2-3   tablespoons olive oil
1   large onion, chopped
1   clove garlic, minced

- In a medium bowl combine ground beef, breadcrumbs, egg white, grated cheese and herbs; mix well and shape into 12 meatballs.
- Heat olive oil and sauté onions and garlic in large non-stick skillet over medium-high heat about 5 minutes; remove from skillet and set aside.
- Brown meatballs in skillet over medium-high heat.
- Add tomato sauce and cooked onions and garlic, cover and simmer for about 15 minutes.

Yields: Approximately 4 servings.

Comments: Serve meatballs in tomato sauce over your favorite pasta. Freeze any leftover meatballs.

Vindicated Veal Roll-Ups

Ingredients:

1½ lbs or 6 veal cutlets, pounded thin
1   clove garlic, minced
2   tablespoons grated Parmesan cheese
1   tablespoon chopped parsley (or basil)
3-4 tablespoons olive oil
½   cup seasoned Italian breadcrumbs
     fresh ground black pepper, to taste
     non-stick cooking spray

- Preheat oven to 350 degrees.
- In a mixing bowl, combine breadcrumbs, grated cheese, parsley, garlic, black pepper and 1 tablespoon olive oil.
- Lay out flat each thinly pounded veal cutlet and place a teaspoon of the breadcrumb mixture in the center of each cutlet.
- Roll up each veal cutlet tightly and secure with toothpicks.
- Line a baking dish with aluminum foil and spray with a non-stick cooking spray; add the rolled veal pieces and drizzle each piece lightly with remaining olive oil.
- Bake approximately 30 minutes.

Yields: 2-3 servings.

Comments: For a quicker version of this dish, pan-sear the veal roll-ups in a tablespoon of olive oil in a large non-stick skillet, instead of baking them. Many thanks to my mother, who made a version of this dish when I was growing up.

"I don't want to know what the law is, I want to know who the judge is."

—Roy M. Cohn

Courthouse Chicken and Rice

Ingredients:

1   cup rice (uncooked)
2-3 tablespoons olive oil
2   large whole boneless, skinless chicken breasts, cut into strips
1   large clove garlic, minced
1   cup sliced zucchini
1   cup red bell pepper strips
1   cup sliced mushrooms
$^1/_3$ cup dry white wine
1½ teaspoons dried Italian seasoning, crushed
4   green onion stalks, cut into strips
$^1/_3$ cup fresh cilantro or basil, chopped
2   tablespoons soy sauce (optional)
     freshly ground black pepper, to taste

- Prepare rice according to package directions. Just before rice is cooked, stir in basil. Drain rice and set aside.
- While rice is cooking, heat oil in a large non-stick skillet. Stir-fry chicken pieces and garlic over medium-high heat for approximately 3 to 4 minutes; stirring quickly and frequently.
- Reduce heat to medium and add to skillet onions, zucchini, red peppers, mushrooms and cook for 2 to 3 minutes.
- Add white wine and cook another 2 to 3 minutes or until vegetables are crispy and tender. Add Italian seasoning, black pepper and soy sauce, if desired.

- Heat all ingredients another 1 to 2 minutes; stirring often.
- Serve over hot cooked rice.

Yields: 2 to 4 servings.

Comments: For a variation of this dish, use any of your favorite vegetables that you happen to have available such as, broccoli, celery, asparagus, and carrots, just to name a few.

Grilled Lemon Herb Chicken

Ingredients:

¼   cup fresh lemon juice
1   tablespoon Dijon mustard
      salt and freshly ground black pepper, to taste
¼   cup extra virgin olive oil
2   whole boneless, skinless chicken breasts, halved
¼   cup fresh parsley or cilantro, chopped
1   large garlic clove, minced and divided
      lemon slices and 1 teaspoon freshly grated lemon zest

For Marinade:
- In a bowl, whisk together lemon juice, mustard, salt, pepper and half the garlic.
- Add oil gradually, whisking until marinade is emulsified.
- Pour marinade over chicken in a large bowl and cover or in a large resealable plastic bag.
- Marinate chicken in refrigerator for at least 1 hour.

Prepare Grill

For Topping:
- In a small bowl stir together remaining garlic, lemon zest and fresh parsley or cilantro.
- Grill chicken on oiled rack about 4-5 minutes each side.
- Serve chicken sprinkled with topping mixture and garnished with thinly sliced lemon slices.

Yields: Approximately 4 servings.

Comments: Cold grilled chicken leftovers also taste great the next day served thinly sliced with a head of romaine lettuce and crusty bread, for a warm weather salad entrée.

Client's Chicken Breasts Florentine

Ingredients:

Nonstick cooking spray and 3 tablespoons olive oil

1   clove garlic, minced
2   cups chopped fresh spinach (or ¼ cup chopped frozen spinach, thawed)
1   cup cooked rice (do not rinse)
2   tablespoons seasoned Italian breadcrumbs
3   tablespoons each chopped fresh basil, and green onions
4   boneless, skinless chicken breasts
    dash of garlic powder, freshly ground black pepper, to taste
3   tablespoons grated Parmesan cheese

- Preheat oven to 400 degrees.
- In a large non-stick skillet add 1 tablespoon olive oil and heat. Add onions, garlic and cook over medium heat 1 minute. Add spinach and cook 2-3 minutes, until spinach is wilted. Place cooked spinach mixture in strainer and press to remove excess moisture.
- In large bowl combine spinach mixture, rice, breadcrumbs, cheese, black pepper, basil and garlic powder.
- Flatten each chicken breast by pounding between two pieces of waxed paper or plastic wrap. Place ¼ of spinach mixture on each breast and roll, tucking in edges to cover filling and secure with toothpicks.
- Heat large skillet with 2 tablespoons olive oil. Add chicken and brown on all sides over high heat for about 3 minutes.

- Remove chicken and place in baking pan coated with nonstick cooking spray and bake for about 10-15 minutes until center is cooked.
- Remove toothpicks and slice chicken into 1 inch thick slices.

Yields: 4 servings.

Comments: This recipe makes a great entrée for entertaining since you can prepare several steps of this recipe (up to the actual cooking of the chicken) ahead of time, so long as you refrigerate and tightly wrap the uncooked stuffed chicken breasts with plastic wrap. When ready to cook the chicken breasts, be sure the chicken breasts have returned to room temperature first, after removing them from the refrigerator, or else the cooking time will be longer.

Civil Crispy Chicken

Ingredients:

4   skinless, boneless chicken breasts (about 4 ounces each)
¾   cup seasoned Italian breadcrumbs
¼   cup grated Parmesan or Romano cheese
     egg substitutes equal to 2 whole eggs
1   tablespoon water
3-4   tablespoons olive oil
     nonstick cooking spray
1   tablespoon fresh chopped parsley, optional
     lemon wedges for garnish, optional

- Preheat oven to 375 degrees.
- In a large bowl, combine breadcrumbs, grated cheese and parsley, if desired.
- In a small bowl, combine egg substitutes and water; mix well.
- Wash and pat dry chicken breasts; then dip each piece in the egg mixture and then coat them in the breadcrumb mixture.
- Line a 13 x 9 inch baking pan with aluminum foil and spray bottom with cooking spray.
- Place breaded chicken into pan and drizzle tops lightly with olive oil.
- Bake chicken uncovered for approximately 35 – 40 minutes until golden brown.
- Turn each piece over halfway through the cooking time for even browning.

Yields: 2–4 servings.

Comments: Serve chicken warm or cold and garnish with lemon wedges, if desired.

The Firm's Fajitas

Ingredients:

several large soft, flour tortillas
1-2 lbs skinless, boneless chicken breasts
2   tablespoons Dijon mustard
4-6 plum tomatoes, cut in half
     a few tablespoons olive oil
1   large bell pepper sliced, cored and seeded
½   cup non-fat sour cream
     chopped green onions for garnish
2   small bunches fresh cilantro
     salt, garlic powder and fresh ground black pepper, to taste
3   large yellow onions, thickly sliced
3   small avocado, optional

Marinade:

Combine lime juice, olive oil, mustard, cilantro, garlic powder, salt and pepper in a small bowl and mix well. Pour marinade over chicken, cover and refrigerate for about 1 to 2 hours.

To Grill:

- Preheat outdoor grill on medium-high heat. Grill marinated chicken several minutes per side until completely cooked through.
- Grill onions, pepper, tomatoes lightly coated with olive oil, for a few minutes per side.

- Lightly oil soft flour tortillas and grill for about 1 minute per side. Watch for burning and remove from grill.
- Garnish the grilled chicken and vegetables with prepared or fresh salsa, green onions, non-fat sour cream and fresh avocado, if desired, and then roll up all ingredients into a large tortilla for each serving.

Yields: 2-4 servings.

"Some circumstantial evidence is very strong, as when you find a trout in the milk."

—Henry David Thoreau

Rapid Ravioli With Tomato Sauce

Ingredients:

1   package (approximately 13 ounces) frozen, large ravioli
2   tablespoons olive oil
2-3 tablespoons fresh basil, chopped
1   small yellow onion, chopped
1   small can diced tomatoes
½   cup water
¼   cup dry white wine
4   fresh, ripe plum tomatoes, diced
1   clove garlic, minced
    freshly ground black pepper, to taste
    grated imported Parmesan cheese, to taste (optional)
    dash of salt, to taste

- Cook ravioli according to package directions.
- While ravioli is cooking: In a large non-stick skillet, heat oil and cook onions and garlic a few minutes until tender. Add canned tomatoes, fresh tomatoes and cook for about 10-15 minutes until fully heated.
- Add water, white wine, basil, salt, black pepper and heat thoroughly for about 10 minutes. Serve over hot freshly drained ravioli.
- Sprinkle each serving with Parmesan cheese, if desired.

Yields: 2 entree servings.

Comments: For a complete meal, serve with some crusty bread and a small green salad on the side.

Libelously Lite Pesto Sauce

Ingredients:

2-3 cloves fresh garlic, peeled

3-4 tablespoons grated imported Parmesan cheese

2 cups fresh basil, washed or 1 cup basil plus 10 ounce package of spinach

¼ teaspoon salt (optional)

¼ teaspoon freshly ground black pepper (or to taste)

1 tablespoon balsamic vinegar

$1/3$ cup non-fat, low-sodium chicken broth

2-4 tablespoons extra-virgin olive oil

• Place the garlic and Parmesan cheese in a food processor or blender.
• Puree for a few seconds.
• Add the basil (or basil and spinach), salt, if desired, black pepper, and balsamic vinegar. Puree again and with the machine running, slowly add olive oil and the chicken broth and puree to make a smooth thick paste.
• Store in the refrigerator in a covered jar for up to two weeks or freeze for up to two months.

Comments: This is a good sauce to make in advance for later use in your favorite dish. Use it as a topping for pasta, or use with grilled or broiled chicken breast or fish. It can also be used as a spread on bread or in baked potatoes as an alternative to butter.

Tortellini With Lite Pesto Sauce

Ingredients:

1   recipe for Lite Pesto Sauce (see recipe)
1   package (about 9 ounces) uncooked tortellini
     or about 6 ounces uncooked angel hair pasta

- Cook the tortellini or angel hair pasta according to package directions. Drain and set aside in a large bowl.
- Add the pesto sauce to the hot pasta and toss lightly until evenly distributed. Do not heat the pesto sauce prior to mixing with the hot pasta. The pesto sauce should be at room temperature prior to mixing with the hot pasta.
- Serve immediately.

Yields: 2 servings.

Comments: Serve with a small green salad and some crusty bread on the side for a complete meal or serve in smaller portions with fresh vegetables, as a side dish to your favorite grilled chicken or seafood dish.

Ethical Eggplant Parmigiana

Ingredients:

2   eggplants, peeled
2   cups skim or non-fat ricotta cheese
    egg substitutes (equivalent to 2 eggs)
¼   cup grated imported Parmesan cheese, plus 1 tablespoon
    salt, for washing eggplant
    freshly ground black pepper, to taste
½   cup basil or parsley, chopped
½   cup light olive oil
2   cups tomato sauce
½   pound skim or non-fat mozzarella cheese, shredded
½   cup seasoned Italian-style bread crumbs (optional)
4   tablespoons skim milk (optional)

- Slice the eggplant into ½ -inch thick pieces and sprinkle pieces lightly with salt in a large bowl and set aside.
- In a mixing bowl, combine ricotta, egg substitutes, Parmesan, basil or parsley and ground pepper.
- Rinse eggplant pieces and pay dry. Set aside.
- Heat a few tablespoons of the olive oil in a large non-stick skillet. Pour milk over the eggplant slices and lightly coat each piece in bread-crumbs, if desired. (For a lighter version of this recipe, omit dipping pieces in milk and coating with breadcrumbs.)
- Sauté a single layer of breaded or plain eggplant pieces a few minutes each side until each side is lightly browned.

- Drain eggplant on paper towels. Put another few tablespoons of oil in skillet and heat. Repeat the process until all eggplant slices are made and drained on paper towels.
- In a 9 x 12 inch baking dish, pour ½ of the tomato sauce and spread over the bottom.
- Arrange a layer of eggplant in bottom of pan and add ricotta mixture in small amounts over eggplants and sprinkle with $1/3$ the amount of shredded mozzarella cheese. Repeat process until all eggplant is used and top final layer with remaining tomato sauce and sprinkle with remaining mozzarella cheese and 1 tablespoon Parmesan.
- Cover baking dish with aluminum foil and bake for 30 minutes in a 400-degree oven.
- Let dish stand for 10 minutes to settle before serving.

Yields: 6-8 servings.

Comments: This makes a good entree to serve when entertaining since it can be made a day ahead and re-heated in the same baking dish covered with foil, when ready to serve. Also, any leftovers freeze well for use at a later date. Try serving this dish with a small serving of your favorite pasta on the side.

Attorney's Appealing Tomato Sauce

Ingredients:

Approximately 4 pounds ripe plum tomatoes, diced
6   ounces tomato paste
2   cups onions, minced
3   tablespoons olive oil
¼   cup fresh basil, chopped finely
¼   cup fresh oregano, chopped finely (or ½ teaspoon dried oregano)
2   cloves garlic, minced
2   tablespoons dry white or red wine
3-4   cups water
      salt & freshly ground black pepper, to taste
      pinch of sugar
2-3   tablespoons Parmesan cheese, grated (optional)

- In a large deep pot, heat olive oil. Add onions and garlic, cook over low heat for about 15 minutes in covered pot. Stir occasionally.
- Add tomatoes, tomato paste, basil, oregano, parsley, salt, pepper and sugar. Stir and simmer for about 15 minutes.
- Add water, wine and simmer slowly over low heat in covered pot for about 1 hour. Stir occasionally.
- Remove cover, stir in grated cheese, if desired, and let sit for a few minutes.
- Use immediately or allow sauce to cool down to room temperature before you cover and refrigerate or freeze for later use.

Yields: Approximately 3 quarts.

Legal Lasagna

Ingredients:

1   lb. (extra lean) ground beef
2   cups tomato sauce
3½   cups part-skim or non-fat ricotta cheese
     egg substitutes equal to 2 eggs
¼   cup fresh chopped basil or 1 teaspoon dried basil leaves
¼   cup fresh chopped oregano or 1 teaspoon dried oregano leaves
8   oz. (1 box oven ready, no boiling) lasagna noodles
3   cups shredded part-skim or non-fat mozzarella cheese
¼   cup grated imported Parmesan cheese (or to taste)

- Preheat oven to 350 degrees.
- In a large non-stick skillet, cook meat until browned; remove from heat. Drain. Stir in tomato sauce with ground meat and heat thoroughly
- In a small bowl, stir together ricotta cheese, egg substitutes, basil, oregano and half of the Parmesan cheese (if desired).
- In a 13 x 9 x 2-inch baking dish, spread ¾ cup meat sauce.
- Place 3 pieces uncooked, oven-ready pasta crosswise over sauce (leaving a space in between each piece since pasta will expand when baked).
- Spread about ²/₃ cup ricotta mixture evenly over pasta. Spread ¾ meat sauce over ricotta; sprinkle with 1 cup mozzarella cheese.
- Repeat the layering process of pasta, ricotta mixture, meat sauce and mozzarella until all pasta is used. Top final layer with meat sauce, mozzarella and sprinkle with remaining Parmesan (if desired).

- Cover dish with aluminum foil. Bake 40-45 minutes. Remove from oven and let stand 10 minutes to settle before cutting.

Yields: Approximately 10 servings.

Comments: This is a great crowd pleasing, make ahead recipe. Prepare as directed, except do not bake. Cover with plastic wrap and foil. Refrigerate up to 48 hours or freeze up to 2 months. Remove plastic wrap; replace foil. Bake refrigerated lasagna as directed above and frozen lasagna about 1 hr 30 minutes. You can also refrigerate or freeze any leftovers.

Roasted Veggie Lasagna

Ingredients:

1   box of ready made lasagna noodles (no boiling required)
16   ounces part-skim or non-fat ricotta cheese
26   ounce jar of tomato sauce (no meat) heated
3   cups shredded part-skim or non-fat mozzarella cheese
1¼   cups grated Parmesan cheese
8-10 fresh large roma tomatoes, cut into 2 inch thick slices
2-3 large yellow or Vidalia onions, peeled and cut into 2 inch
     thick slices
1   eggplant, peeled and cut into 1 inch thick slices
     egg substitutes, equal to 2 whole eggs
     several tablespoons of extra virgin olive oil
     garlic powder, salt and pepper to taste
     bunch of fresh basil and/or oregano, minced

To Roast Veggies:

Preheat oven to 375 degrees. Using 3 separate roasting pans (or cookie sheets) for each of the vegetables, lined with foil, arrange the tomatoes, eggplant and onion slices that have been brushed with a mixture of olive oil, garlic powder, salt and pepper and roast for 20 minutes. (Roast eggplant slices 10 minutes per side, other veggies do not need to be turned.) Remove from oven and cool until room temperature.

For Lasagna Cheese Mixture:
In a large bowl, mix ricotta cheese, 2 cups of mozzarella cheese and ¼ cup of Parmesan with egg substitutes and minced herbs.

To Assemble:
Line bottom of a lasagna pan with approximately 1 cup of tomato sauce. Arrange 3-4 pieces of prepared (no cook) lasagna noodles in bottom of pan, side by side. Next, top each noodle with a layer of cheese mixture, a layer of roasted tomatoes, onions and eggplant. Top with small amount of tomato sauce and add a layer of remaining mozzarella cheese and Parmesan cheese. Repeat steps with another layer of noodles, cheese mixture, veggies and sauce until pan filled. Cover with foil, lower oven temperature to 350 degrees and bake approximately 40-45 minutes. Remove from oven and let stand at room temperature 5 minutes before serving.

Yields: Approximately 6-8 servings.

Comments: In the summer you can make this dish by grilling the veggies on the grill instead of roasting them in the oven.

Substantive Spinach Lasagna

Ingredients:

2   tablespoons olive oil
1   onion, chopped
3-4 garlic cloves, minced
2   (10-ounce) packages frozen chopped spinach, thawed & drained
1½ cups part-skim ricotta cheese
2   cups part-skim mozzarella cheese
1   egg
¼   teaspoon dried oregano
½   cup chopped fresh basil, divided
3   cups prepared marinara sauce
12 pieces dry (oven-ready) lasagna noodles
¼   cup grated Parmesan or Romano cheese
    salt and fresh ground pepper to taste
    fresh chopped parsley (optional)

- Preheat oven to 375 degrees.
- In a large skillet, heat oil over medium heat. Add onion and garlic, and cook until onion begins to wilt, 3-5 minutes.
- Add spinach and half of the basil, stirring until liquid is absorbed, about 5 minutes.
- Remove and spread into a shallow dish.
- In a medium bowl, combine ricotta, mozzarella, egg, oregano, remaining basil, salt and pepper.

- Set aside ½ cup of marinara sauce. In a glass baking pan, pour a thin coating of marinara sauce and cover with 3 uncooked lasagna noodles.
- Top with one third of spinach mixture, followed by one third of cheese mixture.
- Repeat layering process three times.
- Pour on reserved marinara sauce and sprinkle with parmesan cheese.
- Cover dish with foil and bake for 35 minutes. Remove foil and continue baking for 15 minutes.
- Let cool and cut into sections.

Yields: 10–12 servings.

"Laws too gentle are seldom observed; too severe, seldom executed."
—Benjamin Franklin

SIDE BARS:
SIDE DISHES & PIZZA

"Law. A machine which you go into as a pig and come out of as a sausage."

—Ambrose Bierce

"A jury too frequently have at least one member, more ready to hang the panel than to hang the traitor."

—Abraham Lincoln

Easy Zucchini Pie

Ingredients:

4   cups zucchini, finely sliced
¾   cup grated imported Romano or Parmesan cheese
1/3   cup vegetable oil
      the equivalent of 3 whole eggs using non-fat egg substitutes
1   cup chopped mushrooms
1   yellow onion, finely chopped
1¼ cups reduced fat Bisquick baking mix
      freshly ground black pepper and salt, to taste
      garlic powder, to taste

- Preheat oven to 350 degrees.
- Mix all ingredients until well combined.
- Pour mixture into a round 9-inch pie pan or quiche dish or a square baking dish.
- Bake approximately 40 minutes.
- Remove from oven.
- Allow to settle in pan for 15 minutes before serving.
- Serve warm not hot, or allow to cool to room temperature, cover and refrigerate overnight and serve the next day.

Yields: Approximately 6-8 side dish servings.

Comments: This makes a great side dish in place of a starch or as a great brunch dish instead of quiche. It actually tastes better served the next day so you can make this dish ahead. To re-heat, microwave on high 1-2 minutes per slice. Many thanks to my mother, who created a version of this dish, which I have adapted.

Superior Stuffed Mushrooms

Ingredients:

1   small yellow onion, finely minced
1   clove garlic, minced
¼   cup chopped fresh parsley
¼   cup Italian style seasoned breadcrumbs
1-2 tablespoons olive oil, as needed
     freshly ground black pepper, to taste
     imported grated Parmesan cheese, to taste
16   large whole white mushrooms
3   tablespoons fresh basil, minced
     nonstick cooking spray

- Preheat oven to 375 degrees.
- In a nonstick skillet heat olive oil and sauté onion and garlic until just translucent, about 10 minutes. Add parsley, basil and stir for another few minutes. Remove mixture from skillet and pour into mixing bowl. Add breadcrumbs, black pepper, and Parmesan cheese and mix well.
- Wipe mushrooms clean and remove stems but do not discard them. Dice stems finely and add to stuffing mixture and mix well.
- Line a baking dish or cookie sheet with aluminum foil and coat with cooking spray. Set aside.
- Fill each cap with stuffing and pack firmly. Lightly sprinkle tops with additional grated cheese. Sprinkle about a tablespoon or less of olive oil over entire dish of stuffed caps. Bake for 20-30 minutes until well browned.

Yields: About 4-5 appetizer servings.

Comments: Serve these as a side dish with any favorite meat or chicken entree or serve them as an appetizer, at room temperature. Re-heat any leftovers the next day in aluminum foil in a 350-degree oven for about 15 minutes. Thanks again go to my mother, who is the inspiration behind this favorite dish.

Baked Zucchini Sticks

Ingredients:

2　medium zucchini, cut lengthwise and crosswise
1　egg or egg substitutes
½　cup seasoned Italian breadcrumbs
2　tablespoons olive oil
　　non-stick cooking spray
　　a few tablespoons water

- Preheat oven to 400 degrees. Line a baking dish or cookie sheet with aluminum foil and coat with non-stick cooking spray and set aside.
- Wash zucchini and pat dry. Halve zucchini lengthwise and cut crosswise into ½ inch pieces.
- In a mixing bowl, beat egg or egg substitutes with a few tablespoons of water. Dip zucchini pieces into egg mixture one piece at a time, then coat each piece lightly in seasoned bread crumbs.
- Place the breaded zucchini pieces into a prepared baking dish, in a single layer and sprinkle lightly with olive oil on top.
- Bake for approximately 10 minutes on each side or until golden brown. Remove to a plate lined with paper towels before serving.

Yields: About 4 servings.

Comments: These make a great snack or appetizer or serve them as a side dish to any seafood or chicken entree. Note that you can bread these ahead of time and store them covered in the refrigerator until you are ready to bake.

Lawyer's Low-Fat Garlic Bread

Ingredients:

1   loaf Italian bread or 1 French baguette, cut in half lengthwise
6   large cloves garlic
1   tablespoon extra-virgin olive oil
½   teaspoon salt (optional)
      freshly ground black pepper, to taste (optional)

- Preheat oven to 400 degrees.
- Put garlic in a small saucepan with just enough cold water to cover. Bring to a simmer over low heat and cook for 3 to 5 minutes and drain.
- In a small bowl, mash the cooked garlic, oil, salt, and black pepper, with the back of a spoon until a smooth paste forms.
- Spread the mixture over the bread.
- Place the bread on a baking sheet and bake for 10 to 15 minutes, or until the bread begins to turn brown around the edges.
- Slice and serve.

Yields: Approximately 6 servings.

Comments: Serve with your favorite pasta dish or with a green salad.

The Bar's Broccoli and Bowties

Ingredients:

1   bunch of fresh broccoli, stems trimmed and bunch broken into flowerets
2   cloves garlic, minced
2-3 tablespoons extra-virgin olive oil
¼   pound of bowtie pasta
    dash of salt, to taste (optional)
    freshly ground black pepper, to taste

- Cook pasta according to package directions.
- While pasta is cooking, steam broccoli and garlic in about ¼ cup water in a small pan and cover with lid and steam for about 4 to 5 minutes until broccoli turns bright green and is crispy tender.
- Uncover and add 2 tablespoons olive oil, salt, if desired and black pepper, to taste.
- Drain pasta and place in a large bowl. Add cooked broccoli and toss lightly to coat evenly. Add additional salt and pepper, if necessary, to taste.

Comments: This makes a great side dish served in smaller portions or can be served as a meat-less main dish. Re-heat any leftovers the next day in the microwave oven for about 1-2 minutes on high power.

Garnished Garlic Mashed Potatoes

Ingredients:

5   large potatoes, cut into 1-inch cubes (about 7½ cups)
5   whole cloves of garlic, peeled
2   cans (14½ ounces each can) chicken broth
     (low sodium, fat free)
     dash of salt, to taste
     freshly ground black pepper, to taste
¼   cup fresh basil, or chives or Italian parsley, finely
     chopped for garnish (optional)

- In a saucepan place potatoes, whole garlic cloves and broth. Over high heat, heat broth mixture to a boil.
- Cover and cook over medium heat for about 15 minutes or until potatoes are tender.
- Drain potatoes, reserving broth and garlic cloves. Mash potatoes and garlic with 1-1/4 cups broth by hand with large spoon or with mixer or gently in a food processor. Do not over process or else mixture becomes gummy.
- Taste potatoes and season with salt, if desired and pepper, to taste.
- If needed, add additional hot broth to potatoes until desired consistency is reached.
- Garnish with herbs, if desired.

Yields: About 4-6 servings.

Comments: If you like the great taste of garlic, you will love this recipe and never miss the fat, cream and butter found in most traditional mashed potato recipes. The basic garlic-to-potato ratio for this recipe is 1 whole clove of garlic for every potato used.

Rewarding Risotto Verde

Ingredients:

2	cups (low sodium fat-free) chicken broth
1	package (10-ounces) frozen spinach divided
1	tablespoon light butter or margarine
1	tablespoon olive oil
3	tablespoons green onions, minced
1	cup Arborio rice
½	cup dry white wine
1	cup water
½	cup (or to taste) grated imported Parmesan cheese
	salt & freshly ground black pepper, to taste

- Heat chicken broth and keep hot and covered.
- Cook frozen spinach according to package directions.
- In another large saucepan melt butter and add olive oil and heat well. Add onions and sauté a few minutes. Add cooked, drained spinach and mix well. Stir together until all ingredients combined.
- Stir in uncooked rice and stir until it is well coated with mixture. Add wine and stir until wine is completely absorbed.
- Add ¼ the amount of hot broth until there's just enough broth to cover rice. Cook and stir constantly until all liquid is absorbed. Repeat this process several more times until all broth and 1 cup of water has been absorbed a little at a time.

- After about 20 minutes add salt and pepper to taste and the grated Parmesan cheese to taste.
- Turn heat off, cover and let stand a few minutes before serving.

Yields: About 8 servings.

Comments: This makes a great meatless main dish or use as a side dish with your favorite grilled seafood or poultry entrée.

Prosecutor's Potato Fritters

Ingredients:

1   lb. Russet or yellow-flesh potatoes
     equivalent of 2 egg whites or about 3½ ounces of egg substitutes
2-3 tablespoons grated imported Parmigiano – Regiano cheese
2-3 tablespoons minced fresh herbs (such as parsley, oregano, or basil)
1   clove garlic, minced
     dash of salt, to taste
     freshly ground black pepper, to taste
     a few tablespoons olive oil (to cook the fritters)

- Peel the potatoes. Place them in cold salted water and cover in a saucepan. Bring to a boil and cook for about 30 minutes until potatoes are very tender. Drain the potatoes and set aside to cool.
- Put the potatoes through a food mill or grate by hand.
- Combine the potatoes with the egg whites (or substitutes), grated cheese, minced herbs, garlic, salt and pepper, to taste.
- Shape the potato mixture into small balls and flatten each into a disk.
- In a large heated nonstick skillet, heat 1-2 tablespoons of olive oil over medium heat. Cook the potato fritters for about 3-4 minutes per side until golden brown. Add more olive oil, as necessary, to cook the remaining potato fritters.
- Drain on paper towels.
- Serve immediately on a warm plate or keep warm in the oven.

Yields: Approximately 6 small servings.

Grilled Corn Salsa

Ingredients:

1	cob of corn, grilled
1	beefsteak tomato, diced
¼	cup onion, diced
2	tablespoons fresh cilantro, chopped
	juice of 1 lime
2	tablespoons extra virgin olive oil
1	clove garlic, minced
	salt & freshly ground black pepper, to taste

- Remove corn kernels from cob. Combine all ingredients and set aside at room temperature for one hour before serving.

Yields: 2 servings or 1 cup of salsa.

Comments: Try serving this salsa over fresh grilled chicken or seafood dishes.

"Cauliflower is nothing but cabbage with a college education."
—Mark Twain

Appealing Asparagus With Lemon Dressing

Ingredients:

1   pound asparagus spears, (cleaned and ends trimmed)
1   teaspoon minced garlic
1   tablespoon extra virgin olive oil
     salt and fresh ground black pepper, to taste
1   tablespoon grated lemon peel

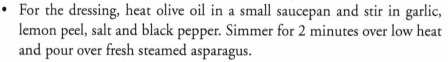

- For the dressing, heat olive oil in a small saucepan and stir in garlic, lemon peel, salt and black pepper. Simmer for 2 minutes over low heat and pour over fresh steamed asparagus.
- To steam asparagus, place ¼ cup cold water in a skillet and bring to a boil. Add clean asparagus spears, cover and steam for 2-4 minutes, until spears are crispy tender and still bright green. Do not overcook asparagus.
- Drain asparagus and serve with Lemon Dressing.

Yields: Approximately 4 servings.

Comments: Versatile asparagus spears make a great side dish to almost any chicken, seafood or meat entrée.

Roasted Asparagus with Breadcrumb Topping

Ingredients:

1   lb. asparagus, uncooked (thicker variety rather than thin aspara-
     gus spears works best here)
¼   cup seasoned Italian breadcrumbs
1   tablespoon extra virgin olive oil
1   tablespoon grated Parmesan cheese
     nonstick cooking spray

- Preheat oven to 400 degrees.
- Line a baking dish or cookie sheet with aluminum foil and spray with nonstick cooking spray. Set aside.
- Wash and trim evenly about ½ inch off ends of asparagus. Pat dry.
- Line asparagus in single layer in lined coated baking dish.
- Combine in a small bowl, the breadcrumbs, grated cheese, olive oil and mix well.
- Sprinkle breadcrumb mixture lightly over raw asparagus. Roast in oven for about 15 minutes (to lightly brown breadcrumb topping). Serve warm.

Yields: 4 side dish servings.

Comments: Thanks again to my mother for inspiring this easy, great-tasting dish.

Grilled Portobello Mushrooms

Ingredients:

4   large Portobello mushrooms (whole not sliced)
3-4 tablespoons extra-virgin olive oil
1-2 teaspoons balsamic vinegar
½   teaspoon Dijon mustard
    salt and fresh ground black pepper, to taste
    dash of garlic powder, optional
    fresh parsley or cilantro for garnish, optional

- Wipe mushrooms clean with damp paper towel, then put them in a large bowl.
- In a small mixing bowl, add vinegar, mustard, salt, pepper and garlic powder, if desired.
- Whisk together ingredients, then slowly add olive oil to vinegar mixture until dressing is fully emulsified.
- Pour dressing over mushrooms and allow them to marinade at room temperature for 30-45 minutes.
- Remove mushrooms from marinade and place them on a pre-heated outdoor grill on medium-high heat for approximately 4 minutes per side, for a total grilling time of 8-9 minutes, depending on size of mushrooms.

Yields: 4 grilled mushrooms.

Comments: Serve them hot off the grill as appetizers or as a side dish with grilled steaks. Garnish mushrooms with fresh parsley or cilantro, if desired.

Residual Rice & Mushroom Stuffing

Ingredients:

¼   cup uncooked wild rice (or 1 cup leftover cooked rice)

8   ounces seasoned stuffing mix

½   lb. panchetta (Italian-style bacon), optional

2   cups non-fat, low sodium chicken broth

2   tablespoons margarine

1   clove garlic, minced

½   cup onion, chopped

½   cup celery, chopped

1   cup sliced mushrooms (portobello, shitake or crimini)

1-2   tablespoons olive oil

     small bunch freshly chopped parsley, basil or cilantro

- Preheat oven to 350 degrees. Cook rinsed wild rice according to package directions and set aside.
- In a large nonstick skillet, cook the panchetta until browned and crispy; drain on paper towel, crumble pieces and set aside.
- Drain off excess panchetta fat from skillet and add a tablespoon or two of olive oil. Cook onions, garlic, celery and mushrooms until very soft; add in fresh chopped herbs.
- In a small saucepan, heat the chicken broth and margarine; bring to a boil. Remove saucepan from heat.
- In a large round casserole, pour in the heated broth; add the stuffing mix, the cooked vegetables, the crumbled panchetta, if desired, and the cooked rice. Mix all ingredients well.

- Cover casserole and bake for 25-30 minutes. For a crispy topping, remove the cover during the last 10 minutes of baking.

Comments: Serve immediately or use to stuff poultry or pork.

"Cheese is milk's leap toward immortality."

—Clifton Fadiman

Prosecutor's Pizza

Basic Pizza Dough
Ingredients:

1   package yeast
1   cup warm water
3½ cups all-purpose flour
1   tablespoon olive oil & 1 teaspoon olive oil, divided
1   teaspoon salt

- In a large mixing bowl, soften yeast in warm water.
- Add 1½ cups flour, 1 tablespoon olive oil and salt to yeast mixture; stir briskly to combine for 3-5 minutes.
- Add remaining flour and stir until dough forms a ball. Remove from mixing bowl and knead, on a floured surface, until smooth and elastic.
- Lightly oil mixing bowl with remaining olive oil, add dough and turn to lightly coat with oil. Cover.
- Let dough rise in a warm place until doubled, approximately 2 hours.
- Next, think of your worst adversary and punch down dough vigorously!

Yields: Basic Pizza Dough for 1 large pizza.

Herb & Cheese Pizza

Ingredients:

1   basic pizza dough (see recipe) or 1 large prepared pizza shell
2   tablespoons olive oil, divided
1   cup tomato sauce
¼   cup fresh herbs, minced (basil and oregano)
1   pound part-skim or non-fat mozzarella cheese, shredded
¼   cup freshly grated imported Parmesan cheese, for topping
     dash of freshly ground black pepper, to taste

- Preheat oven to 400 degrees.
- Lightly coat bottom of pizza pan with 1 tablespoon olive oil. Spread dough out on pan forming thick crust at rim or place prepared pizza shell in pan.
- Top dough or shell, with tomato sauce and herbs. Add shredded mozzarella cheese evenly over pizza dough. Add freshly ground pepper and sprinkle top with Parmesan cheese. Drizzle 1 tablespoon of olive oil over top of pizza.
- Bake for 15-20 minutes on lowest oven rack, then for 5 minutes place on highest rack.
- Remove from oven, wait 10 minutes and slice pizza on cutting board.

Yields: Approximately 4-6 servings.

Roasted Tomatoes & Basil Pizza

Ingredients:

1   basic pizza dough (see recipe)
2   tablespoons olive oil, divided
4-6 plum or roma tomatoes, quartered
¼   cup fresh basil, minced
1   lb. part-skim or non-fat mozzarella cheese, shredded
¼   cup freshly grated Parmesan cheese, for topping
    salt and freshly ground black pepper, to taste

- Preheat oven to 400 degrees.
- Mix tomatoes with olive oil, salt & pepper and place in roasting dish (cut side down).
- Roast tomatoes in hot oven for about 15 minutes or grill tomatoes on an outdoor grill for about 2-3 minutes per side.
- Follow recipe for Herb and Cheese Pizza, except in place of the 1 cup of tomato sauce, use the roasted (or grilled) tomatoes.

Yields: Approximately 4-6 servings.

Witnesses' White Pizza With Veggies

Ingredients:

1   basic pizza dough (see recipe)
2   tablespoons olive oil, divided
3   cups broccoli, cut into small pieces, blanched
1   cup cooked spinach, drained
2   cloves garlic, minced
¼   cup freshly grated Parmesan cheese, divided
       freshly ground black pepper, to taste
½   pound part-skim or non-fat mozzarella cheese, shredded
½   pound part-skim or non-fat ricotta cheese

- Preheat oven to 400 degrees.
- Lightly coat pizza pan with 1 tablespoon olive oil. Spread dough out into pan to form thick crust at rim.
- Spread vegetables evenly over pizza crust. Sprinkle with black pepper and garlic.
- In a small bowl, combine mozzarella, ricotta and one-half the Parmesan cheese. Spread cheese mixture on top of veggies and sprinkle with remaining Parmesan cheese.
- Bake for 15-20 minutes on lowest oven rack, then back on highest oven rack for 5 minutes. Remove from oven and slice pizza on a cutting board. Wait 10 minutes before slicing.

Yields: Approximately 4-6 servings.

"If a man can't forge his own will, whose will can he forge?"
—W. S. Gilbert

CLOSING STATEMENTS:
DESSERTS, MUFFINS & BREADS

"If you can eat sawdust without butter, you can be a success in the law."

—Oliver Wendell Holmes

"The penalty for laughing in the courtroom is six months in jail; if it were not for this penalty, the jury would never hear the evidence."

—H. L. Mencken

Libelously Lite Strawberry Cheesecake

Ingredients:

2 cups graham cracker crumbs
1/3 cup melted margarine
1¼ cups sugar
4 8-ounce packages of non-fat cream cheese product
2 teaspoons vanilla extract
3 whole eggs or equivalent egg substitutes
1 cup non-fat sour cream
1 cup non-fat plain or vanilla yogurt
  *Fresh strawberries for topping

The Crust:
- Combine crumbs, margarine and ¼ cup sugar and mix with fork. Press on bottom and sides of a 10-inch springform pan, and set aside.

The Filling:
- Preheat oven to 350 degrees.
- Using electric mixer at high speed, beat softened cream cheese, remaining sugar and vanilla until creamy.
- Beat in eggs one at a time.
- Blend sour cream in by hand, then blend in yogurt.
- Spread in prepared pan on top of crust.
- Bake for one hour in a larger pan filled halfway with water (water bath prevents cracking).

- Turn oven off, leave door partially open, and leave cheesecake in oven for another one hour.
- Remove spring pan from oven and allow to cool for one hour at room temperature.
- Cover with aluminum foil and chill overnight in refrigerator.
- When ready to serve, remove from refrigerator, release cheesecake from spring pan and top with fresh berries.

Yields: Approximately 10-12 servings.

Comments: For a variation on the topping, use whatever fresh berries are available or a combination of your favorite berries. Since this cheesecake is so creamy and significantly lower in fat than regular cheesecake, it is best used within 1-2 days of baking.

Libelously Lite Pumpkin Cheesecake

Ingredients:

Filling:

4	packages (8 oz. each) non-fat cream cheese product, softened
½	granulated sugar
1	cup light brown sugar
	egg substitutes equal to 3 whole eggs
1	can (15 oz.) pumpkin
1	teaspoon ground cinnamon
½	teaspoon ground ginger
¼	teaspoon ground cloves
1	cup non-fat sour cream
½	cup coarsely chopped walnuts, garnish (optional)

Crust:

2	cups graham cracker crumbs
$1/3$	cup melted margarine
¼	cup light brown sugar

- Combine all crust ingredients together. Press firmly in bottom and up sides of a 10-inch springform pan, and set aside.
- Preheat over to 350 degrees.

- Beat cream cheese until very smooth. Gradually add sugars, beating until well mixed. Add egg substitutes and then add pumpkin, spices and sour cream.
- Pour batter into prepared pan. Bake for 1 hour and 15 minutes.
- Turn over off, leave door partially open, and leave cake in oven for another hour.
- Remove cake from oven and allow to cool at room temperature for one hour.
- Chill cake in refrigerator overnight or several hours before serving. Garnish with chopped walnuts, if desired, prior to serving.

Comments: 10-12 servings.

Fee Simple Fudge Cake

Ingredients:

1	cup unsifted cake flour
1	cup sugar
3	ounces unsweetened cocoa, plus a teaspoon for topping
½	teaspoon baking powder
½	teaspoon baking soda
	dash of salt
½	cup (1 stick) butter or margarine, softened
3	ounces skim milk
¼	cup water
1	egg
1	teaspoon vanilla extract
2	tablespoons Kahlua coffee liqueur or Bailey's Irish Cream
½	cup unsweetened applesauce
½	cup unsalted ground mixed nuts, for topping (optional)

- Preheat oven to 350 degrees. Lightly spray a 9-inch by 3 inch spring-form pan with nonstick cooking spray and set aside.
- Mix flour, sugar, cocoa, baking powder, baking soda and salt in a large bowl. Mix together with an electric beater on low speed for 1 minute.
- Add softened butter, milk, water, egg, vanilla, liqueur and applesauce to dry ingredient mixture. Beat on medium for 1 minute.
- Beat on high speed for 3 minutes until batter is very light and fluffy. Pour into pan. Bake for 35-40 minutes. Cool in pan for 5-10 minutes; remove from pan and cool on rack.

Comments: Pass up the butter cream frosting and instead try grinding up some assorted mixed nuts with a dash of unsweetened coca in a coffee bean grinder for a few seconds and sprinkle over the cake for a nutty flavor.

Associate's Applesauce Coffeecake

Ingredients:

Nonstick cooking spray
2/3 cup plus 1 tablespoon all purpose flour, divided
½ cup plus 1 tablespoon whole-wheat flour, divided
1 teaspoon baking soda
1½ teaspoons ground cinnamon, divided
¼ teaspoon salt
1½ cups finely chopped apples (Granny Smith or Jonathan)
1 egg or ¼ cup egg substitutes
½ cup granulated sugar
½ cup chopped walnuts or pecans, divided
¾ cup applesauce (unsweetened)
¼ cup packed brown sugar
1½ ounces raisins (optional)
1 tablespoon margarine
2 tablespoons (quick cooking type) oats (uncooked)

- Spray a 9 or 10-inch round baking pan with non-stick spray; set aside. In a medium mixing bowl combine 2/3 cup all-purpose flour, ½ cup whole-wheat flour, baking soda, 1 teaspoon cinnamon and the salt; set aside.
- In a large mixing bowl toss together the chopped apple and egg product.
- Stir in the granulated sugar, ¼ cup nuts and the applesauce. Add flour mixture; stir just until combined. Pour batter into the prepared pan.
- For topping, mix together the brown sugar, 1 tablespoon all-purpose flour, 1 tablespoon whole wheat flour and ½ teaspoon cinnamon, cut

in margarine and oats until crumbly. Stir in remaining ¼ cup chopped nuts and the raisins.
• Sprinkle topping over batter in pan. Bake in 350 degree oven for 30-35 minutes. Cool in pan for 10 minutes. Remove pan and serve warm.

Yields: Approximately 8-10 servings.

Comments: This makes a great brunch-type dessert served with coffee or tea.

The Bench's Biscotti

Ingredients:

¾   cup raw, mixed, unsalted nuts (such as filberts, pecans, almonds, cashews, walnuts)

1½   cups whole wheat flour

1½   teaspoons baking powder

¼   teaspoon salt

¼   cup softened butter or 3 tablespoons extra light olive oil (for baking)

½   cup, plus 2 tablespoons granulated sugar

½   teaspoon vanilla extract

½   teaspoon almond extract

½   teaspoon grated orange zest

1   egg

- Preheat oven to 350 degrees.
- Place raw mixed nuts on a baking sheet lined with parchment paper or aluminum foil and toast in the oven for about 5 minutes. Watch for burning. Remove from oven, chop coarsely and set aside to cool.
- Sift together flour, baking powder and salt. Set aside.
- Combine butter or olive oil and sugar and beat on medium speed until light and fluffy. Beat in vanilla and almond extracts, egg and orange zest. Fold in dry ingredients and toasted nuts. Mix until thoroughly blended.
- Line a baking sheet with parchment paper or aluminum foil or spray a baking pan with nonstick cooking spray.

- Shape dough into a 3-by 12-inch mound, with dough formed slightly thicker into the center.
- Bake on middle rack of oven for 18 minutes. Remove pan from oven and reduce oven temperature to 300 degrees. Let cookie loaf cool for 10 minutes in pan.
- Slice loaf on a cutting board, diagonally into ¼ inch slices. Turn slices over so cut side is down. Arrange slices in a single layer in baking pan. Return pan to oven and bake for 10 minutes each side.
- Turn off oven and allow to cool 1-2 hours in oven with heat off.
- Store in airtight container for up to a few weeks.

Yields: About 1 dozen.

Comments: For a variation, you can make chocolate biscotti by adding 4 tablespoons of unsweetened real cocoa to your dry ingredients. Enjoy dunking biscotti into your favorite hot beverage or serve them after a meal and dunk them into Vin Santo, a sweet dessert wine from Italy.

Low-Fat Cinnamon Raisin Scones

Ingredients:

½   cup whole-wheat flour
½   cup all-purpose flour
4   tablespoons brown sugar
1½ teaspoons baking powder
½   teaspoon ground cinnamon
3   tablespoons margarine
1   cup quick cooking rolled oats
    (ground in a blender or food processor)
¾   cup raisins, chopped
2   egg whites or 1 whole egg or egg substitutes
4   tablespoons skim milk

- Preheat oven to 400 degrees.
- Combine flour, sugar, baking powder and cinnamon. Add ground oats, raisins, egg whites or egg substitutes and skim milk. Mix well until dough begins to form.
- On a lightly floured surface, pat dough into a circle the size of a small plate. Slice into 8 wedges (dust knife with flour to prevent sticking).
- Place on an ungreased baking sheet and lightly brush with milk.
- Sprinkle with a little sugar mixed with cinnamon, if desired. Bake for 10 minutes. Cool for 10 minutes on baking rack before serving.

Yields: 8 small scones.

Comments: When baking low fat, remember not to over mix the batter or dough or else the recipe will come out tough and hard. These low-fat scones make a great weekend brunch item or a great snack to enjoy any time served with tea or coffee. To enjoy the next day, re-heat a scone in the microwave oven for about 10 seconds on high power. Store any leftover scones in an air-tight tin or container.

Constitutional Cranberry Corn Muffins

Ingredients:

Nonstick cooking spray
1½ cups all-purpose flour
½   cup fine yellow cornmeal
½   cup sugar (or honey)
4   teaspoons baking powder
½   teaspoon salt
¼   teaspoon baking soda
1   cup non-fat plain or vanilla yogurt
½   cup skim milk
2   tablespoons vegetable oil (or lite butter, melted)
1   egg, lightly beaten
1   teaspoon vanilla extract
1   cup fresh or frozen cranberries

- Preheat oven to 375 degrees, and spray a muffin tin with nonstick cooking spray.
- In a large bowl, combine flour, cornmeal, sugar, baking powder, salt and baking soda.
- In a medium bowl, combine yogurt, milk, oil, egg & vanilla extract. Add the yogurt mixture to the flour mixture. Stir until just combined; do not over mix when baking low fat. Stir in cranberries.
- Spoon batter into prepared muffin tin for 12. Back 20-25 minutes. Cool in pan or on a rack for 10 minutes, then remove muffins from pan and cool on rack.

Yields: 12 muffins, which can be stored frozen for several weeks.

Comments: Blueberries, fresh or frozen, can be substituted for the cranberries.

Plaintiff's Pumpkin Muffins

Ingredients: (Topping)

¼	cup uncooked oats (quick or old-fashioned)
1	tablespoon firmly packed brown sugar
¹/₈	teaspoon pumpkin pie spice

Muffins:

1½	cups all-purpose flour
1	cup oats (quick or old-fashioned)
¾	cup firmly packed brown sugar
2	teaspoons baking powder
1½	teaspoons pumpkin pie spice
½	teaspoon baking soda
½	teaspoon salt (optional)
¼	cup chopped pecans or walnuts (optional)
1	cup canned pumpkin
¾	cup skim milk
2	tablespoons vegetable oil or unsweetened apple sauce
3	egg whites, lightly beaten or one whole egg

- Preheat oven to 350 degrees. Line 12 medium muffin cups with paper baking cups or spray muffin cups with vegetable cooking spray.

For the topping:
- Combine in a small bowl, ¼ cup oats, 1 tablespoon brown sugar and ¹/₈ teaspoon pumpkin pie spice, set aside.

For the muffins:
- Combine in a large bowl the flour, remaining oats, remaining brown sugar, baking powder, remaining pumpkin pie spice, baking soda, salt and nuts; mix well. In a medium bowl combine pumpkin, milk, oil and egg whites; mix well. Add to dry ingredients; mix just until moistened. [Do not over mix or these lower-fat muffins will be tough.]
- Fill muffin cups almost full; sprinkle evenly with topping. Bake 22-25 minutes. Cool muffins 5 minutes in pan on wire rack; remove from pan. Serve warm.

Yields: 1 dozen muffins.

Licensee's Lemon Muffins

Ingredients:

2	cups all-purpose flour
½	cup granulated sugar
1	tablespoon light brown sugar, optional
2	tablespoons poppy seeds
1	tablespoon baking powder
1	teaspoon baking soda
1	tablespoon grated lemon zest
$1/_8$	teaspoon salt
1¼	cups lemon nonfat yogurt
¼	cup canola oil
	egg substitutes equal to 2 whole eggs
4	tablespoons fresh lemon juice
	nonstick vegetable spray

- Preheat oven to 375 degrees. Spray a muffin pan with nonstick vegetable spray and set aside.
- In a large bowl, combine flour, sugar, poppy seeds, baking powder, baking soda, lemon zest and salt.
- In a medium bowl, combine yogurt, oil, egg substitutes, and lemon juice; whisk smooth.
- Pour yogurt mixture into flour mixture and stir until just combined, do not over mix (batter should be slightly lumpy).
- Spoon into prepared muffin pans and bake approximately 25 minutes.

Yields: 12 muffins.

Comments: These muffins can be made ahead and stored in the freezer for up to 1 month. Thawed muffins can be reheated in a 350-degree oven for 5-6 minutes.

Banana Nut Bread

Ingredients:

$^1/_3$ cup fruit based fat substitute or unsweetened applesauce (or 1 stick softened light butter)

¾ cup sugar

2 whole eggs

2 large ripe bananas, mashed

1¾ cups all-purpose flour

1 teaspoon baking powder

1 teaspoon baking soda

½ teaspoon salt

1 teaspoon vanilla extract

½ cup chopped walnuts or pecans (optional) nonstick cooking spray

- Preheat oven to 350 degrees. Spray a loaf pan with nonstick cooking spray and set aside.
- Beat fruit based fat substitute or applesauce (or light butter) with sugar until smooth. Add eggs one at a time and continue beating. Beat in vanilla extract. Fold in mashed bananas.
- Sift dry ingredients in a large bowl. Add all the dry ingredients to the banana mixture. Stir gently just to combine and add nuts last, if desired.
- Pour mixture into loaf pan. Bake approximately 40 minutes, until golden brown. Remove from oven.
- Cool in pan for 10 minutes before removing to a cooling rack.

Yields: 1 large loaf.

Comments: Try a slice for breakfast with low-fat cream cheese on top.

Zealous Zucchini Bread

Ingredients:

1	cup sugar
1	tablespoon light brown sugar
¾	cup applesauce, unsweetened
1	cup whole-wheat flour
½	cup all-purpose flour
1	teaspoon each baking powder, baking soda, salt and cinnamon
1½	cups shredded raw zucchini
1	teaspoon vanilla extract
2	whole eggs or egg substitutes

- Preheat oven to 350 degrees. Lightly coat a loaf pan with non-stick cooking spray. Set aside.
- Mix sugars and applesauce in a bowl. Combine dry ingredients and add to applesauce mixture. Add zucchini and vanilla.
- Beat eggs slightly and add to mixture. Mix until well combined but do not overmix.
- Pour into loaf pan and bake for 45 minutes.
- Remove from oven. Cool in pan for 10 minutes and then cool on wire rack for another 10 minutes before slicing and serving.

Yields: About 12 slices.

Comments: This makes a great light dessert served with tea or coffee, or can be added to your favorite weekend brunch menu. You can also cut the loaf in half and freeze in aluminum foil while you use the other half.

"Equity does not demand that its suitors shall have led blameless lives."

—Louis Brandeis

Bailiff's Blueberry Drop Biscuits

Ingredients:

2   cups reduced fat biscuit baking mix (such as Pioneer or Reduced Fat Bisquick brands)

¾   cup skim milk

½   cup fresh blueberries, washed and pat dry

- Preheat oven to 400 degrees.
- In a large mixing bowl, stir together the baking mix and milk just until a soft, moist dough begins to form. Do not overmix.
- Add blueberries to mix last and stir in gently. Do not knead dough since these are drop biscuits.
- On an ungreased baking sheet, drop biscuit mixture by tablespoon onto the baking sheet.
- Bake for 10 minutes. Do not overcook or else bottoms will burn.
- Serve warm.

Yields: 10 biscuits.

Comments: These biscuits are really quick and taste best when they are just made and served warm. If you do not need 10 biscuits at one time, just cut the recipe in half to make 5 fresh biscuits. You can also substitute your favorite berries such as raspberries, blackberries or cranberries in place of the blueberries. Frozen berries in the batter also work just as well as fresh berries.

Barrister's Brownies

Ingredients:

Nonstick cooking spray
$1^1/_3$ cups all-purpose flour
$1^1/_3$ cups granulated sugar
½   cup unsweetened cocoa powder
¼   cup cornstarch
1   teaspoon baking powder
1   teaspoon baking soda
½   teaspoon salt
$^2/_3$ cup prune puree (see recipe below or use a fruit-based
     fat substitute such as applesauce or Light Bake brand)
3   egg whites
1   cup cold coffee
1   tablespoon vanilla extract

- Preheat oven to 350 degrees. Coat a 9-inch baking pan with cooking spray.
- In a large bowl or in an electric mixer bowl, combine flour, sugar, cocoa powder, cornstarch, baking powder, baking soda and salt.
- In a medium bowl, beat prune puree (or other fruit-based fat substitute) and egg whites to blend thoroughly. Gradually beat in coffee and vanilla.
- Pour wet ingredients into dry ingredients. Beat just to blend thoroughly. Do not overbeat.

• Pour into pan. Bake for about 30 minutes. Cool on rack. Cut into 3-inch squares.

Yields: 9 servings.

Comments: This recipe is adapted from a California Prune Board recipe. In place of the prune puree, you can also use jars of baby food prunes.

For Prune Puree: Combine $1^{1}/_{3}$ cups (8 ounces) pitted prunes and 6 tablespoons hot water in container of food processor or blender. Pulse or blend on and off until prunes are finely chopped. Cover and refrigerate up to 1 month.

Yields: 1 cup.

Common-Law Carrot Cake

Ingredients:

1	cup sugar
1	tablespoon light brown sugar
¾	cup applesauce, unsweetened (or other fruit-based fat substitute)
1	cup whole wheat flour
½	cup all purpose flour
1	teaspoon baking powder
1	teaspoon baking soda
1	teaspoon ground cinnamon
½	teaspoon salt
2	cups finely shredded raw carrots (use food processor)
1	teaspoon vanilla extract
¼	cup chopped walnuts (optional)
2	eggs (or egg substitutes)
1½	ounces (about 1 small snack size box) raisins

- Preheat oven to 350 degrees. Lightly coat a loaf pan with non-stick cooking spray. Set aside.
- Mix sugars and applesauce in a bowl until well combined.
- Combine all dry ingredients and add to applesauce mixture. Mix in vanilla. Add carrots, raisins and walnuts, if desired.
- Beat eggs lightly and add to mixture until well combined. Do not overmix.
- Pour mixture into loaf pan. Bake for 45 minutes in a 350-degree oven.

• Cool in pan for 10 minutes before slicing and serving.

Yields: About 12 slices or 1 loaf.

Comments: If you don't need a whole loaf, cut loaf in half, wrap in aluminum foil and freeze. Makes a great breakfast or weekend brunch bread or if desired, serve as a light snack or dessert, with Cream Cheese Frosting (see recipe).

Credible Cream Cheese Frosting

Ingredients:

8 ounce bar of fat free cream cheese product, softened to room temperature
½ cup or less, to taste, powdered sugar
½ teaspoon vanilla extract
½ teaspoon ground cinnamon

- Beat with electric mixer, the cream cheese and powdered sugar until well combined.
- Add the vanilla and cinnamon and beat thoroughly.
- Adjust amount of sugar and cinnamon to taste.

Yields: Enough to frost 1 carrot cake.

Comments: When serving carrot cake as a breakfast or brunch item, omit the frosting and serve plain or with a low-fat cream cheese spread. Serve with the frosting when serving the carrot cake as a dessert or snack.

Attorney's Apple Pie

Ingredients:

6 to 8   small Granny Smith (or any tart) apples,
       pealed and thinly sliced
½   cup light brown sugar, firmly packed
2   tablespoons cornstarch
2   tablespoons softened light butter or margarine
1   teaspoon cinnamon
½   teaspoon coriander
2   frozen 9 inch unbaked pastry shells
    juice of ½ lemon
1   teaspoon finely grated lemon rind

- Preheat oven to 400 degrees.
- Toss sliced apples with lemon juice and rind.
- Combine cornstarch, light butter or margarine, brown sugar, cinnamon and coriander. Toss with apple mixture.
- Spoon mixture into pastry shell. Take second pastry shell and place it inverted over the top of the filled pastry shell. Slightly moisten the edges with water to shape into place. Pierce small air holes with a fork or knife into the top pastry shell before baking.
- Bake for 15 minutes. Reduce temperature to 350 degrees and continue baking for 30-35 minutes longer until it turns golden brown.
- Remove from oven and allow pie to cool at least 30-45 minutes before serving.

Comments: Serve with a low-fat vanilla ice cream or frozen yogurt sprinkled with cinnamon, if desired or serve plain. Store any remaining pie in the refrigerator.

Supreme Strawberry Rhubarb Pie

Ingredients:

2   cups fresh strawberries, sliced
1   lb. fresh rhubarb, cut into 1-inch pieces
     (approximately 3½ cups)
1¼   cups granulated sugar
½   cup all-purpose flour
2   tablespoons fresh lemon juice
1   teaspoon ground cinnamon

Crust:
Two refrigerated, prepared 9-inch deep-dish pie crusts

- Preheat oven to 400 degrees.
- In a large bowl, combine strawberries, rhubarb, sugar, flour, lemon juice and cinnamon. Spoon mixture into bottom of one 9-inch refrigerated pie crust that's been pre-cooked and placed in a pie or quiche pan. Cut up second pie crust (uncooked) into 1-inch wide strips and place over pie lengthwise and then across the top creating a lattice type design.
- Bake until golden and filling is bubbly, about 45-50 minutes. Transfer to a wire rack.

Yields: 6-8 servings.

Comments: Serve warm or at room temperature. Top with non-fat vanilla ice cream, or frozen yogurt, if desired. By pre-cooking the piecrust before pouring in the fruit mixture, you can avoid a soggy bottom fruit pie.

Partner's Pumpkin Pie

Ingredients:

1   (9-inch) unbaked pastry shell
2   (15-ounce) cans pumpkin
2   (14-ounce) cans low-fat sweetened condensed milk
3   egg whites or egg substitutes or 2 whole eggs
1   teaspoon ground cinnamon
½   teaspoon ground nutmeg
½   teaspoon salt
     chopped walnuts for garnish (optional)

- Preheat oven to 425 degrees.
- In a large mixing bowl, combine all ingredients, except pastry shell and mix well.
- Pour mixture into pastry shell.
- Bake 15 minutes. Reduce oven temperature to 350 degrees, and bake 25 to 30 minutes longer or until knife inserted into center comes out clean.
- Cool. Garnish by sprinkling top with chopped walnuts, if desired. Refrigerate leftovers.

Yields: 8-10 servings.

Comments: This reduced fat version of the classic Thanksgiving Day dessert has 36% less fat than the traditional recipe, but has all the great taste of the original version.

"A fruit is a vegetable with looks and money. Plus, if you let fruit rot, it turns into wine, something Brussels sprouts never do."
                                                            —P. J. O'Rourke

Berry Lite Trifle

Ingredients:

1	quart vanilla non-fat yogurt
½	quart light or non-fat whipped cream
1	pint strawberries (whole, stemmed)
1	pint blueberries (whole)
½	pint raspberries (whole)
½	pint blackberries (whole)
2	kiwi fruit (sliced in ¼ inch slices)
1	angel food cake or low-fat pound cake
	a few tablespoons, rum (to taste) or Chambord raspberry liquor

To Assemble:

• Crumble the cake and using about ¼ the amount, create a first layer (in a large glass trifle bowl) by sprinkling cake crumbs with rum (or Chambord) until evenly moistened. Next, add layers of yogurt, fruit and cake, repeating until the bowl is filled.

• Garnish with whipped cream and slices of kiwi. Chill in refrigerator for about 2 hours before serving, for trifle to set.

Yields: Approximately 10-15 servings. [For a small trifle bowl, use ½ the amount of ingredients.]

Comments: This makes a quick and elegant warm weather dessert when your favorite fresh berries are in season.

Felonious Fruit & Creamy Yogurt Dip

Ingredients:

4	cups low-fat or nonfat, vanilla or plain, yogurt
¼	cup firmly-packed, dark brown sugar
	assorted fresh fruits, cubed
2	tablespoons low-fat granola, garnish (optional)

- Combine yogurt with sugar in a small bowl and stir together until thoroughly blended and smooth.
- Cover and refrigerate until ready to serve.
- Serve dip with cubed assorted fresh fruit and garnish serving bowl with granola, if desired.

Yields: 4 cups of creamy dip.

Comments: This makes a great tasting low-fat snack for the warm weather season or try serving this as part of a brunch buffet.

Pleasing Poached Pears

Ingredients:

3½   cups water
½   cup orange juice
½   cup granulated sugar
1   lemon peel twist or 2 teaspoons minced orange zest or
     fresh mint leaves
6   large pears
2   tablespoons orange liqueur or raspberry liqueur

- Combine water, orange juice and sugar in a large saucepan; bring to a boil. Pare the pears and trim slightly to level bottom. Remove cores leaving stems intact.
- Add pears to poaching liquid; reduce heat. Cover and simmer gently about 8-10 minutes or until tender. Turn and baste occasionally. Remove pears, reserving poaching liquid. Cool on flat dish.
- Add either lemon twist or orange zest or fresh mint leaves, to reserved poaching liquid. Boil uncovered for 20 minutes, until liquid is reduced to about 1 cup.
- Stir in liqueur. Spoon flavored warm mixture over cooled pears. Chill until served.

Yields: Approximately 6 servings.

"To succeed in other trades, capacity must be shown; in the law, concealment of it will do."

—Mark Twain

ABOUT THE AUTHOR

"Wherever we are, it is but a stage on the way to somewhere else. And whatever we do, however well we do it, it is only preparation to do something else that is different."

—Robert Louis Stevenson

Flavia Joyce Tuzza is a lawyer and a gourmet food enthusiast, who received her law degree from Syracuse University's College of Law. She received her undergraduate degree from Fordham University. A native of New York, she took the New York Bar Exam and practiced law in New York City with a small litigation firm, where the partners in the firm gave her something to laugh about almost everyday.

Thereafter, to reunite with the love of her life (a non-lawyer), she relocated to the Atlanta area, overcame culture shock and then took the Georgia Bar Exam in 1986, where she continued to practice law, primarily in the area of commercial real estate.

Over the years in Atlanta, Flavia has worked in law firms (both small and large) where she developed her keen sense of humor, and also spent several years as an in-house attorney for the federal government, where she further developed her keen sense of humor. Flavia has also spent a few years practicing law as a contract attorney, which has given her the opportunity to work in-house for the private corporate sector while giving her the flexibility to tap into her creative side.

All during her stints in private practice, with the government and in the corporate sector, Flavia enjoyed cooking light and healthy recipes with thoughts of one day writing a fun cookbook targeted to the legal community. For Flavia there was only one possible name for such a project, **LegalEats, A Lawyer's Lite Cookbook**. She took a sabbatical from the practice of law, enjoyed a short trip to Italy for further inspiration and then came home with a renewed desire to complete and bring **LegalEats** to life.

Flavia is a member of the State Bar of Georgia and the New York State Bar. She currently resides in the Atlanta area with her husband, Ira Gleser, the marketing/business guru who gets to try all her new recipes firsthand.

"The great thing in this world is not so much where we are, but in what direction we are moving."

—Oliver Wendell Holmes

INDEX

74563389R00116

Made in the USA
Lexington, KY
15 December 2017